Dignity as a Human Right?

Dignity as a Human Right?

George P. Smith, II

LEXINGTON BOOKS
Lanham • Boulder • New York • London

Published by Lexington Books
An imprint of The Rowman & Littlefield Publishing Group, Inc.
4501 Forbes Boulevard, Suite 200, Lanham, Maryland 20706
www.rowman.com

6 Tinworth Street, London SE11 5AL, United Kingdom

British Library Cataloguing in Publication Information Available

Library of Congress Cataloging-in-Publication Data Available
ISBN: 978-4985-8419-7 (cloth : alk. paper)
ISBN: 978-1-4985-8420-3 (electronic)

™ The paper used in this publication meets the minimum requirements of American National Standard for Information Sciences—Permanence of Paper for Printed Library Materials, ANSI/NISO Z39.48-1992.

Printed in the United States of America

Honoring Three Lifetime Mentors

To the Honorable Michael D. Kirby, formerly Justice of the High Court of Australia, whose vision and eloquence in championing human rights enkindled my interest in this critical area, and provided me with personal and professional fulfillment.

For Dr. Edmund D. Pellegrino, Georgetown University School of Medicine, who encouraged, nurtured, guided, and inspired my work in bioethics and in health law.

For Professor William W. Bishop, Jr., University of Michigan Law School, who showed me as a student and as a young scholar, the all-encompassing force for good of international law.

Contents

Preface

Dignity is seen commonly as an ethical obligation owed to human persons. The dimensions of this obligation in today's postsecular society are, however, subject to wide discussion and debate, for the term "human dignity," and its preservation, defy universal agreement. Since dignity is incapable of being "operationalized,"[1] it is argued that it cannot be recognized as a policy standard. Indeed, in the United States, there has simply been "no coalescence . . . around the rational possibilities that exist for a legal theory of human dignity."[2] Thus, the legal ontology of dignity lies in obfuscation.[3]

Yet, even with these negative arguments against the recognition and the application of dignity as a normative value, America has nonetheless chosen to base its sociolegal and ethical understanding of dignity on a libertarian tradition—this, being contrary to some European countries who anchor dignity to notions of paternalism or communitarism.[4] Dignity is acknowledged as the United States Constitution's fundamental value and the "cardinal principle for which the Constitution stands."[5] It remains an open question whether dignity is considered properly as an integral component of the very concept of personhood, derived, as such, from autonomy, equality, or liberty, or whether it is an independent attribute of personhood.[6]

Critical contemporary issues of dignity, and challenges to it through indignity, prejudices, and negative stereotyping, have complex sociolegal scenarios running the gamut from LGBTQ and transgender issues[7]—including hormone therapy[8] for gender re-assignment cases, both for those in everyday society and those who are incarcerated[9]—to the disabled,[10] the elderly,[11] the mentally retarded,[12] religious dissidents,[13] and the dying.[14] It is this last class, and particularly efforts to manage death in a humane and dignified manner, which will be examined and tested in order to discern the parameters of dignity and the consequences of not providing it. Within clinical medicine, safeguarding the dignity of the patient is the core responsibility of all physicians, and with this responsibility comes a co-ordinate obligation to not only respect patient autonomy but to undertake actions with beneficence and non-maleficence.[15]

Complicating the challenge to the science of medicine to promote and maintain dignity for those at the end-of-life is a startling prediction by the Centers for Disease Control that by the year 2050, some 138 million Americans will have Alzheimer's disease[16]—with the average life span for such patients being eight to ten years.[17] The costs of clinical care for patients with this disease and other forms of dementia are calculated to have been $259 billion in 2017.[18] More than two-thirds of these costs are covered by Medicare and Medicaid.[19] A report from the Alzheimer's Association in 2010 placed the cumulative costs of care for people with this disease exceeding $20 trillion by 2050.[20]

All too often, dementia patients and others suffering with the infirmities of old age live in an "existential vacuum," and seek death because they have lost the meaning of life. In other words, depression and hopelessness prevent them from developing an "ability to experience meaning,"[21] which is the primary motivational force in humans.[22] When medically futile health conditions of this nature are diagnosed as such, the question then becomes the extent to which medicine should accord assistance and secure dignity for those with who have refractory physical pain and existential misery and who have exhausted their supply of a "strength to live."[23] Instead of experiencing catharsis, as occurs when a patient emerges from illness and progresses to rehabilitation,[24] there is simply no patient catharsis here because there is neither emergence from, nor rehabilitation of, medical conditions deemed futile. It is well to remember that the very same minimal conditions that are so vital for a life of dignity (e.g., autonomy, compassion, decency, humanness, respect, and well-being), are the same conditions which are exactly in play when managing death.[25]

While foundational instruments of international law such as the Universal Declaration of Human Rights, the International Covenant on Economic, Social and Cultural Rights, and the Covenant on Civil and Political Rights, as well as the Universal Declaration on the Human Genome and Human Rights, together with the Convention on Human Rights and Biomedicine, all codify a mandate to ensure human dignity within various contexts of international conduct, the notion—itself—is stated normally in grandiloquent terminology without more and always subject to progressive realization rather than absolute recognition.[26]

The spirit of constitutional nationalism following World War II evidenced a strong effort among a number of nation-states to establish dignitarian "rights" and protections within their constitutions.[27] This effort has had a salutary effort in providing a framework within which coordinated international activity can be orchestrated. Indeed, ongoing international efforts must continue to be taken in order to guide the actions of states in seeking to set and to maintain levels of cultural and social conduct that serve to safeguard human dignity throughout life[28] and especially at its end-stage. Without issues of justiciability being resolved, and the absence of a central enforcement, however, dignity will likely remain an elusive fact-sensitive value—but certainly not, in and of itself, a cognizable normative standard.

Rights are defined and examined within the context of society and not individually.[29] Thus, neither the individual nor the societal groups within which there is interaction are pivotal; rather, it is the association between these two which gives meaning and depth.[30] The existence of both is dependent upon the other—for, "individuals cannot exist apart from the group, and the group cannot persist without its individual members."[31] The principle of subsidiarity, thus, plays out richly when rights are placed and tested within the ambit of international rights and responsibilities.[32]

By definition, human rights law centers on the human being, the subject of rights and the nature of "the good" persons require to flourish in "their exercise of free moral agency."[33] In order to achieve this level of living, persons need "not only an immunity from certain kinds of harms or violations of their dignity" but also under certain circumstances "an affirmative form of assistance and intervention."[34]

The sentiments of the Honorable Michael D. Kirby, formerly Justice of the High Court of Australia, and one of the foremost international jurists of the day, both capture and synthesize the judicial concerns with the use of dignity as a normative value when he states: "Dignity tends to be a conclusionary notion and not one that provides a clear criterion by which to judge compliance or non-compliance."[35] Furthermore, "it conjures up different things in different cultures. Thus, for Western cultures, respecting a person's privacy and thus, right to sexual expression, would be seen as part of their dignity as human beings. But, in . . . other cultures [such as Asian and African ones] such notions are completely alien and are resisted."[36]

Even with these valid reservations by Justice Kirby, the noble goal of fostering and preserving standards for dignity, together with the prevention of indignity, must continue to be an ever-present value, guiding principle, normative "standard," if not ideally even a human right, in the vast plethora of dignitary issues within the global community. At a minimum, human dignity and the goal of its use and implementation can serve as an invaluable catalyst for not only informing, but shaping, ongoing debates on this exceedingly complex and vital issue of concern. Principles of international equity might even be seen as a supportive template for assessing and validating actions, which secure dignity and well-being in health care decision-making at the end-stage of life.[37]

NOTES

1. David A. Hyman, *Does Technology Spell Trouble with a Capital T: Human Dignity and Public Policy*, 27 HARV. J. L. & PUB. POL'Y 3, 17 (2003).

2. Rex D. Glensy, *The Right to Dignity*, 43 COLUM. HUM. RTS. L. REV. 65, 107 n. 202 (2011). *See* Ruth Macklin, *Dignity Is a Useless Concept*, 327 BR. MED. J. 1419 (Dec. 20–27, 2003) (holding that dignity could well be eliminated in medical ethics altogether and concluding that, in actuality, appeals to dignity are used to promote patient autonomy in end-of-life treatment decisions). *See also* Stephen Pinker, *The Stupidity of Dignity*, NEW REPUBLIC at 1, May 28, 2008 (stating dignity is a "squishy, subjective action" and its use in law is analytically and seriously confused).

3. David Weisstub, *Honor, Dignity, and the Framing of Multicultural Values*, is THE CONCEPT OF HUMAN DIGNITY IN HUMAN RIGHTS DISCOURSE 263, 270–71, 274 (David Kretzner & Eckart Klein eds., 2002). *But see* Jeremy Waldron, *How Law Protects Dignity*, 71 CAM. L. J. 200 (2012) (asserting the inherent character of law is to deal with human persons as dignified agents).

4. Glensy, *supra* note 2.

5. *Trop v. Dulles*, 356 U.S. 86, 100–02 (1998). Analogous to the abstruse nature of dignity, is the issue of how to give morality meaning in the field of human rights. One approach to this quandary is to identify, define, and apply morality by reference to national constitutions where interpretative frameworks can be developed and used to explicate various concepts of morality within human rights instruments. Ryan Thoreson, *The Limits of Moral Limitations: Reconceptualizing Morals in Human Rights Law*, 59 HARV. INT'L L. J. 197, 229–32 (2018). For an illuminating listing of moral provisions in international and regional instruments, see pages 240–44. *See generally* George P. Smith, II, *Dignity in Living and in Dying*, 25 INDIANA J. GLOBAL LEGAL STUDIES 413 (2018).

6. Glensy, *supra* note 2. Interestingly, the very scope of dignity widens when considered within the context of property law and the specific issue of dignity takings and restoration are analyzed—with such takings occurring whenever the state confiscates or destroys property from individuals which de-humanize them. *See* Symposium, *Dignity Takings and Dignity Restoration*, 92 CHI-KENT L. REV. 713 (2017).

7. Neo Khuu, *Comment, Obergefell v. Hodges: Kinship, Formation, Interest Convergence and the Future of LGBTQ Rights*, 64, U.C.L.A. L. REV. 184 (2017). *See* Michael Boucsi, *Is Assisted Procreation an LGBT Right?* 2016 WISC. L. REV. 1065. *See also* Alan K. Simpson, *Don't Let the Anti-LGBT Bigots Win*, N.Y. TIMES, Mar. 20, 2017 at 27; Arne Duncan, *Protecting Transgender Students Is Our Federal Responsibility*, WASH. POST, Feb. 24, 2017 at A7.

8. Silpa Maruri, *Hormone Therapy for Inmates: A Metonym for Transgender Rights*, 20 CORNELL J. L. & POL'Y 807 (2017). *See* Matt Apruzzo, *Transgender Inmate's Hormone Treatment Lawsuit Gets Justice Department Backing*, N.Y. TIMES, April 3, 2015, at 1.

9. Alexander Kirkpatrick, Note, *The Caged Bird Sings of Freedom: Why Allowing Sex-Reassignment Surgery for Transgender Life Prisoners Facilities Rehabilitation*

and Reconciliation, 26 S. CAL. REV. L. & SOC. JUST. 37 (2016). *See also* Amy Ellis Nutt, *John Hopkins Resuming Transgender Surgeries*, WASH. POST, April 6, 2017, at 1 (reporting how these surgeries, which had been banned for thirty-eight years because "no objective advantage [was found] in terms of social rehabilitation," have begun anew).

10. Harlan Hahn, *Antidiscrimination Laws and Social Research on Disability: The Minority Group Perspective*, 14 BEHAVORIAL SCI. & L. 41 (1996).

11. AI-JEN POO, THE AGE OF DIGNITY: PREPARING FOR THE ELDER BOOM IN A CHANGING AMERICA (2015).

12. George P. Smith, II, *Just Say No! The Right to Refuse Psychotropic Medication in Long-Term Care Facilities*, 13 ANNALS OF HEALTH L. 1 (2004). *See* T. L. Scheid, *Employment of Individuals with Mental Disabilities: Business Response to the ADA Challenge*, 17 BEHAVIORIAL SCI. & L. 73 (1999).

13. CARL W. ERNST, ISLAMPHOBIA IN AMERICA: THE ANATOMY OF INTOLERANCE (2013). *See* Lauren Sudeall Lucas, *The Free Exercise of Religious Identity*, 64 U.C.L.A. L. REV. 54 (2017).

14. George P. Smith, II, PALLIATIVE CARE AND END OF LIFE DECISIONS (2013). *See* Smith, *supra* note 5.

15. GEORGE P. SMITH, II, *Cura Personalis: A Healthcare Delivery Quandary at the End of Life*, 7 ST. LOUIS U. J. HEALTH L. & POL'Y 311 (2014). See George P. Smith, II, *Gently Into the Good Night: Toward a Compassionate Response to End-Stage-Illness*, 22 TEMPLE U. J. POLITICAL & CIVIL RIGHTS 475 (2013). *See generally* GEORGE P. SMITH, II, *The New Biology and Biotechnology*, Ch. 8 (1989).

16. Ariana Eunjung Cha, *Alzheimer's Death Rate is Rapidly Rising in U.S.*, WASH. POST, May 20, 2017, at A15.

17. *See* http://www.healthline.com/health/alzheimers-disease/life-expectancy#overview. Susan L. Mitchell et al., *The Clinical Course of Advanced Dementia* 361 NEW ENG. J. MED. 1529 (Oct. 15, 2009).

18. Cha, *supra* note 16.

19. *Id.*

20. *See* www.alz.org/trajectory. *See generally* MARTIN ROTH, AGEING AND THE AGED IN CONTEMPORARY SOCIETY (1993).

21. EMILY SMITH, THE POWER OF MEANING: CRAFTING A LIFE THAT MATTERS 220 (2017).

22. *Id.* at 226.

23. ANDRZEJ SZCZEKLIK, CATHARSIS: ON THE ART OF MEDICINE at 87 (2005). *See* George P. Smith, II, *Safeguarding Autonomy and the Prohibition against Cruel and Unusual Punishment*, 12 J. CONTEMP. HEATH LAW & POL'Y 1 (1996).

24. SZCZEKLIK, *id.* at 143.

25. WALTER KÄLIN & JORG KÜNZLI, THE LAW OF INTERNATIONAL HUMAN RIGHTS PROTECTION 303 (2004).

26. *See* Ch. 7, *infra*. *See also* Appendices B, C & D, *infra*.

27. AHARON BARAK, HUMAN DIGNITY: THE CONSTITUTIONAL VALUE AND THE CONSTITUTIONAL RIGHT (2015). *See generally*

RETT LUDWIKOWSKI & GISBERT H. FLANZ, HUMAN RIGHTS AND FUNDAMENTAL FREEDOMS (2002).

28. *See generally* Neomi Roo, *On the Use and Abuse of Dignity in Constitutional Law*, 14 COLUM. J. EUROPEAN L. 201 (2008). The extent to which the state seeks to merge human relationships within the family unit and particularly children, may well be shaped by reliance on human dignity as a normative value. Securing the "best interests" of the child are realized, then, when the family unit itself is respected and protected. Peggy Cooper Davis, *Little Citizens and Their Families*, 43 FORDHAM URB L. J. 1009 (2016).

29. CHRISTOPHER N. J. ROBERTS, THE CONTENTIOUS HISTORY OF THE INTERNATIONAL BILL OF HUMAN RIGHTS 230 (2014).

30. *Id.*

31. *Id. See* Jeremy Waldron, *supra* note 3 (asserting human rights laws involve the protection of dignity and/or the prevention of degradation). *See generally* LON L. FULLER, THE MORALITY OF LAW (1964).

32. *See* John Finnis, *Subsidiarity's Roots and History: Some Observations*, 61 AM. J. JURIS. 133 (2016).

33. Paolo G. Carozza, *The Problematic Applicability of Subsidiarity to International Law*, 61 AM. J. JURIS. 51, 54 *passim* (2016).

34. *Id.*

35. June 16, 2017, email from Justice Kirby to the author.

36. *Id. See generally* Michael D. Kirby, *Human Rights—The Challenge of The New Technology*, 60 AUSTRALIAN L. J. 170 (1986).

37. *See* Ch. 7, *infra*. *See also* George P. Smith, II, LAW AND BIOETHICS: INTERSECTIONS ALONG THE MORTAL COIL, Ch. 8 (2012).

Acknowledgments

Serious research and writing for this book began during the summer of 2013 with a research appointment to the Lauterpacht Research Centre for International Law, University of Cambridge, England. This scholarship continued during the summer of 2014, with an affiliation at the Petrie-Flom Center for Health Law, Policy, Biotechnology, and Bioethics at Harvard Law School. Two subsequent affiliations provided continued opportunities for research and writing: one at the Institute for Advanced Study, Indiana University, Bloomington, in the autumn 2016, and one at the Solomon Center for Health Law and Policy at the Yale Law School during the summer of 2017.

Some of the ideas in this book are drawn from three articles that I authored: *Dignity as a Normative Standard or as a Value in Global Healthcare Decision Making?*, 42 North Carolina Journal of International Law 275–305 (2017); *Human Rights and Biomedicine: Formulating a Universal Right to Health, Health Care or Health Protection?*, 38 Vanderbilt Journal of Transnational Law 1295–1323 (2005) and *Refractory Pain, Existential Suffering, and Palliative Care: Releasing an Unbearable Lightness of Being*, 20 Cornell Journal of Law and Public Policy 469–532 (2011); and, from four lectures that I delivered: "Dignity in Living and in Dying," the Henry Remak Memorial Lecture, Indiana University, March, 2017; "Dignity in Dying: Ubiquitous, Capacious, or Normative?," Faculty of Law, Oxford University, March, 2014; "Seeking an Easeful Death: Emanations within a Penumbra," the Rothermere American Institute, University of Oxford, March, 2014; and "Bioethics and Human Rights: Toward a New Constitutionalism," the George Winterton Memorial Lecture, University of Sydney, Australia, August, 2010.

Chapter 1

Challenges to the Notion of Dignity as a Human Right

Acknowledged as a notion that neither exists in today's society nor is a proper description of the world, human dignity is nonetheless accepted as possibly "the premier value underlying the last two centuries of moral and political thought.[1] The degree to which law accommodates dignity is evolving[2] as the precise mean of human dignity can only be tested within the context of specific factual (e.g., situational) settings.[3]

As a moral term, dignity suggests how individuals should or should not be treated individually or as a group within a given social and cultural grouping.[4] Accordingly, no acceptable standard working definition of dignity is applicable uniformly.[5] At a minimum, dignity means "respect for the intrinsic worth of every person."[6]

TAXONOMIES AND PRAXIS

Having a loose definitional form results in varying definitions of dignity and acts of interpretations. Under one definition, dignity is viewed as a collective virtue,[7] which may function as a "substantive positive right," a "background interpretative norm," a "proxy device," or as "hortatory language."[8] Seen as a substantive right, abridgements of dignity are actionable against an individual as well as the government.[9] Another popular view holds dignity is magnified within the law as equality, liberty, and personal integrity.[10] Perhaps rather than being seen as a basic moral concept or even a normative standard, a type of functional utility for dignity is to be found in its capacity to further an ongoing basic dialogue through the development and use of a common language where both values and rights—when in conflict—"can be brought into a relationship with each other."[11]

Grounded in the concept of autonomy by Kant, acknowledged as the father of the concept, itself, dignity was cast as a normative legal ideal.[12] Nations have either chosen to relate human dignity to the status of a foundational right supporting all other rights, or alternatively paired it with rights to equality and of liberty.[13] Within the second paragraph of the Preamble of the Charter of the United Nations, human dignity appears as an ideal that "the peoples of the United Nations" are "determined" to achieve—this, by reaffirmation of their "faith in fundamental human rights, in the dignity and worth of the human person, in the equal rights of men and women and of nations large and small.[14]

The noble and lofty ideal of dignity allows easy acceptance and affirmation, but being nearly devoid of a substantive context. The application of it as a normative standard is much akin to the test Justice Potter Stewart set in 1964 for determining something was obscene. Using a commonsense subjective standard, Justice Stewart said, famously, that he knew obscenity when he saw it.[15] Indeed, Oscar Schachter opined that while violations of human dignity were difficult to determine, they could nonetheless be assessed by using the epistemology of, "I know it when I see it even if I cannot tell you what it is."[16] Perhaps a similar commonsense, intuitive approach or even a consensus morality[17] to assessing dignity—and practices of indignity—could be used in evaluating cases of misconduct in managing end-of-life care.

In an effort to quantify conduct, which degrades human dignity, various lists have been compiled of conduct and ideas that are "implicitly incompatible with the basic ideas of the inherent dignity and worth of human persons."[18] Among some twelve levels of conduct which challenge the notion of dignity are: "degrading living conditions and deprivation of basic needs"; "statements that demean and humiliate individuals or groups because of their origins, status or belief"; and "medical treatment or hospital care insensitive to individual choice or the requirements of human personality."[19] Central to the very ideal of human dignity, then, are modes of conduct and ideas antithetical or incompatible with respect for basic or inherent dignity.[20]

VARYING INTERPRETATIONS

The principle of human dignity is considered differently among historians, philosophers, theologians, and lawyers.[21] There is no uniform agreement emerging from these groups. Yet, there is a level of consensus acknowledging that this principle, at its core, accepts the intrinsic value of all human beings,[22] and that it cannot be lost or forfeited. Politically, the principle of human dignity stands for the proposition that "the state exists for the sake of individual human beings.[23]

Historians, without taking any position as to how the principle of human dignity is either understood or dismissed as invalid, recognize this principle as "an evolving theme in the history of ideas."[24] Philosophers either accept the principle as a moral norm, which must be explored as to its "content, validity and consequences" or, alternatively, as either a "delusion or deceit."[25] Theologians ponder the principle as a "proposition about the relationship between human beings and God."[26] Lawyers perceive the principle of human dignity "as a positive legal norm in a particular legal system"[27] which must be either constructed or, as necessary, deduced.[28]

The foundation of the law of human rights is the principle of human dignity—for, recognition of this value supports the reason "to construct a system of legal rights" designed to protect individuals—by asserting positive rights—against actions which are inconsistent with human dignity.[29] Inasmuch as human rights treaties, national constitutions and global resolutions are born of the political process,[30] the meaning of the term and the legal content of human dignity, then, varies from nation-state to nation-state.[31] "Translation across boundaries" is a constant and vexatious reality in international diplomacy.[32] Yet, the noble goal of transnational instruments has been—and will always remain—to advance and safeguard the notion of the universality of protection of human dignity for "all persons under all governments in all societies."[33]

SUPPORTING THE FOUNDATIONAL NORM

While human dignity is—within the system of international human rights—regarded as a foundational norm, it is often used as an applicable norm for setting standards of conduct which are allowed.[34] Examples of this approach are to be found within the International Covenant on Civil and Political Rights and the International Covenant on Economic, Social, and Cultural Rights, which are designed to give "legal force to the aspirational Universal Declaration of Human Rights."[35]

Since the legal content of human dignity may very well vary from one national constitutional system to another, it is obvious to conclude that the substance of the norms of human dignity will also vary regionally "as between more inclusive and more circumscribed" systems for human rights.[36] Even though the legal conception of the universality of human dignity must be applied within each system, differences in their legal conceptions within the systems may be in play giving rise to issues of subsidiarity.[37]

Interestingly, although there is no operative provision referring expressly to human dignity found within the European Convention for the Protection of Human Rights and Fundamental Freedom, which entered into force in 1950, still—when interpreting the Convention, the concept of human dignity is employed routinely.[38] The reason given for this exclusion was that since human dignity was an underlying value in the Convention, itself, it would be superfluous to state it explicitly.[39] Subsequently, in 2001, the European Court followed the momentum set previously by the European Court of Human Rights and held that human dignity had pre-eminence of recognition as a "legal value underlying the European Convention."[40] Specific clarity was achieved in 2009 when the Treaty of Lisbon entered into force and, for the first time, gave a normative definition of human dignity which, in turn, became binding on the European Union and its member states when implementing the laws of the European Union.[41] Previously, in 2000, the Union's Charter of Fundamental Rights both recognized in its preamble the "universal values of human dignity," and in Article 1 declared, "Human dignity is inviolable. It must be respected."[42]

Another way of addressing human dignity issues is done routinely by acceptance of "neutrally stated norms" at the national level, which has the effect of allowing constructs to be framed in order to reach a "European consensus." This then serves as a *modus operandi* for interpreting and settling issues raised under the European Convention.[43]

In addition to dignity being acknowledged as a foundational value in the law of human rights, there are other primary values that may be considered as being "inherent in or intrinsic to common humanity." These values are autonomy, self-respect, and equality.[44] Common humanity may be seen as "the humanity of human beings," which is, in other words, "their humanity within the society in which they live."[45] This humanity is one "which is built on mutual relationships"—not only "between the individual and other individuals" but also between "them and the state."[46] At the very heart of what it means to preserve self-respect or self-worth is found the need to protect against insult and humiliation.[47]

From the dignitary right, it has been suggested that a number of derivative (un-enumerated) "daughter" rights arise and include: the rights of personality; family life; equality; freedom of expression; freedom of conscience and religion; freedom of movement; education; employment; and to due process.[48]

DIGNITY IN DEATH

It is within the very issue of death management that human dignity is tested, both as to parameters of personal dignity and to basic dignity.[49] Indeed, within end-of-life care, dignity can be seen correctly as a human rights issue.[50] In everyday conversation, dignity at death means the avoidance of "being helpless, incontinent, dependent, drooling, a burden to others and of poor general deportment."[51]

A powerful interface exists between the right to human dignity and the right to life; for, "many of the claims to a right to die with dignity actually reaffirm a more general commitment to life (including life shared, love, and humanity) and to the ending of one's life in dignity."[52] In this sense, "*an affirmation of human dignity, its strength and grandeurs, is an affirmation of the eternity of life*."[53] These fundamental human rights reflect, plainly, the interrelated right to a basic quality of life and, additionally, "in the rights to adequate food, health care, and shelter recognized in Article 25 of the Universal Declaration."[54] Inasmuch as death is a part of life, "choice concerning life must necessarily include choice concerning the end and ending of life."[55]

Included within the right to human dignity must be "a right to live with dignity, and thus a right to end one's life without indignity—indeed, a right not to be compelled to live the remainder of life in indignity."[56] When remaining life has any quality and yields indignity, it is both humane and efficacious to respect "the dignity of personal choice."[57]

Although no express right to die with dignity is to be found in definitive instruments on human rights,[58] the very Charter of the United Nations addresses the need to protect and safeguard the essential "dignity and worth of the human person."[59] "The inherent dignity . . . of all members of the human family" is recognized in the preamble of the Universal Declaration of Human Rights.[60] And, the Declaration states further that not only are "[a]ll human beings are born free and equal in dignity and rights," but that each is entitled to have both respect and value, and to a right to dignity.[61] An interrelated right of privacy is, furthermore, recognized in Article 12 of the Declaration.[62] Even though phrased as a qualified right, it is nonetheless viewed correctly as extending in scope to include all personal choices such as those regarding death and dying.[63]

NOTES

1. Rex D. Glensy, *The Right to Dignity*, 43 COLUM. HUMAN RIGHTS L. REV. 65, 72 nn. 32, 33 (2011). *See* IN DEFENSE OF HUMAN DIGNITY: ESSAYS FOR OUR TIMES (Robert P. Kraynack & Glenn Tinder eds., 2013).

2. Glensy, *id.*

3. *Id.* at 67, n. 11. A perennial clash over the issue of whether there is a difference between ethics and morality often finds common understanding in accepting the assertion that the former tests the rightness or wrongness of conduct while morality deals with the degree of evil accompanying conduct. For bioethical decision making, the goal is "to do the right thing," or—in other words —the "moral thing." To that end, then, conduct which "directs one's will in accord with the human good" is the situational goal to be achieved in issues of human dignity. Richard John Neuhas,

Human Dignity and Public Disclosure, in Human Dignity and Bioethics: Essays Commissioned by the President's Council on Bioethics 215, 216 (2008) [hereinafter HUMAN DIGNITY AND BIOETHICS]. *See* Edward J. Eberle, *Human Dignity, Privacy and Personality in German and American Constitutional Law*, 1997 UTAH L. REV. 963, 975.

4. FIONA RANDALL & R. S. DOWNIE, END OF LIFE CHOICES: CONSENSUS AND CONTROVERSY 178 (2010).

5. *Id.* at 179.

6. Glensy, *supra* note 1 at 72. *See generally* DIGNITY, CHARACTER, AND SELF RESPECT (Robert S. Dillon ed., 1998). Dignity and respect have a symbiotic or interdependent relationship—if not actually being conjoined—because, while everyone is born with inherent values and worth, respect is earned. DONNA HICKS, DIGNITY: THE ESSENTIAL ROLE IT PLAYS IN RESOLVING CONFLICTS (2011).

7. Glensy, *supra* note 1.

8. *Id.* at 142.

9. *Id.* at 111.

10. *See* Leslie M. Henry, *The Jurisprudence of Dignity*, 160 U. PA. L. REV. 169 (2011).

11. Christopher McCrudden, Ch. 1, *In Pursuit of Human Dignity: An Introduction to Current Debates*, at 14 in UNDERSTANDING HUMAN DIGNITY (Christopher McCrudden ed., 2015 [hereinafter UNDERSTANDING DIGNITY].

12. Glensy, *supra* note 1 at 76. Kant's notion of "humanity in dignity," which belies the very basis of all conceptions of human rights, does not however hold true—*ipso facto*—in practice "that all human beings have certain rights simply by virtue of being humans." The possibility of this normative ideal becoming a practical norm depends upon legal "formulation and prescription." James Orbinski, *Justice and Global Health* in 16 LAW AND GLOBAL HEALTH at 11 (Michael Freeman, Sarah Hawkes & Belinda Bennett eds., 2014). *See generally* Jordan J. Paust, *Human Dignity as a Constitutional Right: A Jurisprudentially Based Inquiry into Criteria and Content*, 27 HOWARD J. 145 (1984); Joel Feinberg, *The Nature and Value of Human Rights*, 4 J. VALUE INQUIRY 243, at 252–53 (1970) (holding dignity as a normative value).

13. Glensy, *supra* note 1 at 69. *See* GEORGE P. SMITH, II, HUMAN RIGHTS AND BIOMEDICINE (2000). *See also* James Q. Whitman, *The Two Western Cultures of Privacy: Dignity Versus Liberty*, 113 YALE L. J. 1151 (2004).

14. Paust, *supra* note 12. *See* Preamble, *Charter of the United Nations*, 1945, www.un.org/en/documents/charter/. *See* Appendix A, *infra*.

15. *Jacobellis v. Ohio*, 378 U.S. 184, 197 (1969), (Stewart, J. concurring).

16. Oscar Schachter, *Human Dignity as a Normative Concept*, 77 AM. J. INT'L. L. 848, 849 (1983).

17. David N. Weisstub, *Honor, Dignity, and The Framing of Multiculturalist Values*, 263 at 244 in THE CONCEPT OF HUMAN DIGNITY IN HUMAN RIGHTS DISCOURSE, hereinafter, CONCEPT OF HUMAN DIGNITY (David Kratzmer & Eckart Klein eds., 2002).

18. Schachter, *supra* note 16 at 852. Inasmuch as kindness in healthcare settings is seen as affecting patient outcomes and levels of satisfaction, it is now being "taught" in today's medical schools. The closest medical researchers have come to promoting kindness as a basic health value is found in and through acts of empathy. Although still unclear what the result of a "lack of a linear response to empathy" may be manifested, there is recognition that "kindness carries with it a commitment to a certain way of thinking and being rather than to a particular pre-defined endpoint." Michael Stein, *Does Kindness Actually Help Us Get Well?* WASH. POST, Aug. 14, 2016, at B1. *See generally* MICHAEL STEIN, THE LONELY PATIENT (2007).

19. *Id. See also* Aurel Kolnai, Dignity, 51 PHILOSOPHY 251 (1976). *See also* Alexander M. Capron, *Indignities, Respect for Persons and the Vagaries of Human Dignity BMJ Rapid Responses*, Dec. 31, 2003 (available online at http://bmjjournals.com/agi/eletters/327/7429/1419).

20. Kolnai, *id.* at 852. Although recognizing various types of dignity, it has been suggested, nevertheless, that there is a commonality among all notions of dignity—namely, the use of this word to reference a property or properties "that cause one to excel, and thus elicit or merit respect from others." Patrick Lee & Robert P. George, *The Nature and Basics of Human Dignity*, at 410 in HUMAN DIGNITY AND BIOETHICS, *supra* note 3.

21. Gerald L. Neuman, Ch. 38, *Discourses of Dignity in Understanding Dignity*, *supra* note 11.

22. *Id.* at 638.

23. *Id.*

24. *Id.*

25. *Id.*

26. *Id.*

27. *Id.*

28. *Id.*

29. *Id.*

30. *Id.* at 639–42.

31. *Id.* at 642. *See* Rhoda E. Howard & Jack Donnelly, *Human Dignity, Human Rights and Political Regimes*, 80 AM. POL. SCI. REV. 801 (1986).

32. Neuman, *supra* note 21 at 642.

33. *Id.* at 645.

34. *Id.* at 641.

35. *Id.* at 643. *See* Christopher McCrudden, *Human Dignity and Judicial Interpretation of Human Rights*, 19 EUROPEAN J. INT'L L. 655, 667 *passim* (2008). For listings of human dignity as used in human rights texts see 664 *passim*; in U.N. documents at 667; and in regional texts at 671 *passim*, McCrudden, *id.*

36. Neuman, *supra* note 21 at 646.

37. *Id. See* Vicki C. Jackson, *Constitutional Dialogue and Human Dignity: State and Transnational Constitutional Disclosures*, 63 MONT. L. REV. 1 (2004).

38. Neuman, *supra* note 21 at 646.

39. AHARON BARAK, HUMAN DIGNITY: THE CONSTITUTIONAL VALUE AND THE CONSTITUTIONAL RIGHT at 54–55 (2015).

40. Neuman, *supra* note 21 at 646–67. The Court of Justice of the European Union is not related to the European Court of Human Rights. *See* ELSPETH GUILD & GUILLAUME LESIEUR, THE EUROPEAN COURT OF JUSTICE ON THE EUROPEAN CONVENTION ON HUMAN RIGHTS (1998).

41. *See* http://eur-lex.europa.eu/legal-content/EN/TXT/?uri-celex%2A12007L%2FTXT. *See also* Catherine Dupre, Ch. 5, *Constructing the Meaning of Dignity: Four Questions* at 113 in UNDERSTANDING DIGNITY, *supra* note 11 at 117–18. The first mention of dignity, specifically, in a normal text, was in 1848 in a French degree prohibiting slavery. *Id.* at 117.

42. *See* http://www.europa.eu/charter/pdf/text_en.pdf.

43. Neuman, *supra* note 21 at 647.

44. Jerry L. Mashaw, *Administrative Due Process: The Question of a Dignity Theory*, 61 BOSTON U. L. REV. 885, 908 (1981).

45. Aharon Barak, Ch. 20, *Human Dignity: The Constitutional Value and The Constitutional Right* at 369 in UNDERSTANDING HUMAN DIGNITY, *supra* note 11.

46. *Id.*

47. Doron Shultziner & Itai Rabinovici, *Human Dignity, Self-Worth and Humiliation: A Comparative Legal-Psychological Approach*, 18 PSYCHOLOGY, PUB. POL'Y & L. 105, 128 *passim* (2012).

48. AHARON BARAK, *supra* note 39 at 288–301. *See* MATTHIAS LUTZ-BACHMANN, HUMAN DIGNITY AND COSMOPOLITAN IDEAS (2013).

49. David C. Thomasma, *The Principle of Dominion*, 133 at 137–38 in THE HEALTH CARE PROFESSIONAL AS FRIEND AND HEALER: BUILDING ON THE WORK OF EDMUND D. PELLEGRINO (David C. Thomasma & Judith Lee Kissell eds., 2000). *See* Paul Ramsey, *The Indignity of Death with Dignity*, 2 HASTINGS CENTER STUDIES 47 (May 1974).

50. RANDALL & DOWNIE, *supra* note 4 at 178. *See* Jordan J. Paust, *The Human Right to Die with Dignity: A Policy-Oriented Essay*, 17 HUM. RTS. Q. 463 (1995).

51. JANET L. DOLGIN & LOIS L SHEPHERD, BIOETHICS AND THE LAW 484 (3rd ed., 2013). New research, drawn from 180 hospital patients over the age of 60, either approaching or under imminent peril of death regarding their attitudes toward functional debility, found certain conditions more unbearable than death itself. The ranking of these conditions in descending order were: bowel and bladder incontinence; reliance on breathing machines in order to live; immobility and confinement to bed; confusion and the need for constant care; dependence on feeding intubation; living permanently in a nursing home; confinement to home living; consistent moderate pain; confinement to a wheelchair. Letter, Emily B. Rubin, Anna E. Buehler et al., *States Worse than Death among Hospitalized Patients with Serious Illness*. Online August 1, 2016, at doi:10.1001/amainternmed.2016.4362. *See* A GOOD DEATH? LAW AND ETHICS IN PRACTICE (Lynn Hagger & Simon Woods eds., 2013). *See also* ATUL GAWANDE, BEING MORTAL (2014) (forcefully arguing for greater acceptance of palliative care and hospice care as alternatives to seeking death with dignity by embracing assisted suicide or euthanasia).

52. Paust, *supra* note 50 at 480–81. *See* Peter T. Struck, DIVINATION AND HUMAN NATURE: A COGNITIVE HISTORY OF INTUITION IN CLASSIC ANTIQUITY (2016) (showing that "surplus knowledge"—or intuition, allows knowledge of certain things without understanding how a judgment is made). *See generally* BRANDY SCHILLACE, DEATH'S SUMMER COAT: WHAT THE HISTORY OF DEATH AND DYING CAN TELL US ABOUT LIFE AND LIVING (2015).

53. Paust, *supra* note 50 at 480–81.

54. *Id.* at 486. *See generally* George P. Smith, II, Ch. 24, *Global Health Law: Aspirational, Paradoxical, or Oxymoronic?* at 24 in LAW AND GLOBAL HEALTH, CURRENT LEGAL ISSUES (Michael Freeman, Sarah Hawkes & Belinda Bennett eds., 2014).

55. Paust, *supra* note 50 at 480–81.

56. *Id.* at 480–81. *See generally* GEORGE P. SMITH, FINAL CHOICES: AUTONOMY IN HEALTH CARE DECISIONS (1989).

57. Paust, *supra* note 50 at 480–81.

58. *Id.* at 476.

59. U.N. G.A. Res. 217A, U.N. Doc. A/810, at 51 (1948). *See* Appendix A, *infra.*

60. *Id.*

61. *Id.*

62. *Id. See* Appendix B, *infra.*

63. Paust, *supra* note 50 at 477.

Chapter 2

The Origins and History of Human Dignity

RELIGIOUS, PHILOSOPHICAL, AND ETHICAL FOUNDATIONS

Although not in the classical world regarded as inherent to all individuals, the notion of dignity or human worth was recognized in early history—but only for virtuous persons.[1] Consequently, orphans, slaves, and those with physical defects were excluded altogether from qualifying for an ascription of being entitled to dignity.[2]

The early views of the Jewish and the Christian faiths ascribed to the idea that all human beings were made to the image and likeness of God.[3] This concept subsequently grew into the acceptance of the premise that the body and the soul were to be seen as integrated.[4] And, this understanding of *Imago Dei*, or the image of God, in all of God's creations, provided the foundation for the belief that there was an intrinsic value in each of those who bore his image.[5]

Interestingly, the word "dignity" derives from the Latin *dignitas* (i.e., worth) and *dignus* (worthy). When applied to *homo sapiens*, this etymology implies that every individual must be acknowledged as imbued with an inherent value and, accordingly, be treated with proper respect.[6] Much of a contemporary understanding of human dignity can be attributed to religion and to ancient civilizations.[7] Indeed, human rights—comparable to ones enumerated in modern international instruments—also have a clear provenance in history and biblical faith; for, within equality, concern for the poor and social justice are to be found the very seeds of human rights and the dignity of man.[8]

Kantian Influence and the Roman Catholic Church

Kant's moral philosophy—and particularly his theory of rights—at first glance, may improperly lead to a conclusion that morality and dignity are "interchangeable terms."[9] Stated succinctly, the Kantian theory recognizes that persons "receive the respect they deserve as ends," when they are treated in a "way that shows respect for the moral law," and not when morality is mimicked "out of one or another emotion or interest, much less when we immorally or disrespectfully use them as mere means."[10] For Kant, respect for the moral law is accorded by actions, while "respect for persons as ends" is shown by the dealings had with them," which, in turn, are seen as an "unbreakable knot."[11]

Kateb cautions that if additional bases "for respecting human beings and hence their rights," are recognized[12] rather "than their capacity to act morally," then, "the moral and the existential" should not be held as "interchangeable terms"[13] nor as "tied into an unbreakable knot"[14]—especially since "free agency is a broader concept than moral agency."[15] In addition to respect for the moral law, other praiseworthy sources of moral conduct may be found in pit or compassion.[16]

Papal Leadership

Within the community of world religions, a consistently strong leadership role in securing the dignity of personhood can be claimed properly by the Roman Catholic faith.[17] Pope Leo XIII (1810–1903), is his encyclical, *Rerum Novarum*, authored in 1891, established for Catholic social teaching, the idea of the "dignity of labor,"[18] which, understood properly, was "less an assertion of equality than an expression of the view that labor should be given its proper place within a social order."[19] This premise was developed further and refined in Pope Pius XI's encyclical, *Quadragesimo Anno*, or, the Reconstruction of the Social Order, in 1931, where dignity was recognized as being central to an all-encompassing Catholic social thought. *Pacem in Terris*, 1963, written by Pope John XXIII, solidified the place of dignity in relation to establishing universal peace in truth, justice, charity and liberty.[20] There the pope declares:

> Man has the right to life. He has the right to bodily integrity, and to the means necessary for the proper development of life . . . he has the right to be looked after in the event of ill-health.[21]

Dignity, as within the right to human well-being, was a significant principle in Pope Paul VI's encyclical, *Populorum Progressio* (On The Progress of Peoples) authored in 1967 as well as in Pope St. John Paul II's *Centesimus Annus*, written in 1991 on the hundredth anniversary of *Rerum Novarum*, which presented a modern perspective on the social teachings of the Church and, while defending private property, insisting on imposing social limits to this right.[22]

Pope John Paul II, in his Apostolic Letter *Salvifici Doloris*, issued February 11, 1984, spoke eloquently of the essentiality of "every individual to 'stop,' as the Good Samaritan did, at the suffering of one's neighbor, to have 'compassion' for that suffering and to give some help."[23] The pope urged the cultivation of a "sensitivity of heart" which—in turn—"bears witness to compassion toward a suffering person,"[24] and to an understanding that humans should be treated "as a psychological and physical whole."[25] His Holiness, Pope Benedict XVI, in remarks made on March 30, 2006, observed that today, as in the past, the principle focus of interventions by the Catholic Church have been to protect and to promote the dignity of the person, both from "moment of conception until natural death."[26] And, in 2015, Pope Francis declared December 8, 2015–November 20, 2016, to be a Holy Year of Mercy, and observed that in all actions, mercy should be considered before judgment because "everything in our lives is a gift, everything is mercy."[27]

Milbank cautions that while papal encyclicals and other Catholic writings on social teaching adopt the concept of rights in liberal Kantian terms, at the same time, they suggest a foundation in autonomy—with dignity being seen as either supplemental or even as redundant.[28] It is speculated that not until after World War II, Catholic social teaching accepted, fully, the notion that dignity entailed both social and political equality and, furthermore, that dignity was, indeed, "connected with the idea of inviolable human rights."[29]

FUNDAMENTAL OR COMPETING RIGHTS?

The modern genesis of human rights is to be found in the United Nations 1948 Universal Declaration of Human Rights,[30] together with the 1966 International Covenant on Civil and Political Rights,[31] and International Covenant on Economic, Social and Cultural Rights.[32]

By their very nature, human rights are inherent to all individuals and not dependent upon the state for either their existence or their enjoyment.[33] This Universal Declaration of Human Rights proclaims this basic principle when it acknowledges that "All human beings are born free and equal in dignity and rights."[34] The function of human rights, then, is to create state obligations, and not to create general ethics.[35] Human rights are seen properly as setting not only minimum standards for governance but as a means for safeguarding against state oppression.[36] Indeed, these rights "are at the heart of a free and democratic society."[37]

While the Universal Declaration is non-binding, significant parts have attained the status of binding—rules of customary international law or, alternatively, are acknowledged as part of those general principle of law subscribed to by civilized nations.[38] It has been said, in fact, that the enumerated rights set forth within the Declaration are "made whole by dignity."[39] In and of themselves, the principles enumerated within the Declaration are not human *rights*. Respect for human dignity is the catalyst for a human rights policy whenever freedom and equality are jeopardized.[40]

Human Rights and the Rights of Man

The provenance of The Universal Declaration of Human Rights is to be found within the ideas and philosophies of the eighteenth-century Enlightenment, the American and French revolutions, together with the movement toward democracy and of liberalism.[41] "On the surface, they reflect the democratization and universalization of values and norms which have always been held as a supreme, existential importance by men, tribes, nations, the world over and by the ruling classes at least in the West."[42] Central to the notion of citizenship, for the Greeks through the ideal of the *Politeia* and by the Romans in the *civis romanus*, were the core values of liberty, dignity, and self-determination[43]; just as in the same fashion that it was asserted by European societies and the nobility.[44]

The theory of the "Rights of Man" was, then, drawn from past beliefs, as well as traditions and experiences by the intellectual leaders of the West.[45] In fact, this bold contention was the basis for proclaiming the inalienable rights of citizens in the U.S. Declaration of Independence[46] and, to a degree, the substance of the American national identity[47] and value system.[48]

POST–WORLD WAR II CONSTITUTIONAL PROTECTIONS

Most national constitutions included no recognition of dignity before WWI, which started in 1914.[49] Dignity, as a constitutionally recognized, value appeared after the end of the war in 1918 for the first time in Finland's Constitution of 1919 when it recognized that each Finnish citizen would have life, dignity, personal liberty, and property protected.[50] The Constitutions of the Weimar Republic of Germany in 1919, together with Estonia 1920, Lebanon 1926, Ecuador 1929, Ireland 1937, and Nicaragua in 1939, were notable in their early efforts to, at one level or other, acknowledge human dignity as a protected value or right.[51]

After the conclusion of WW II in 1945, a new impetus of importance was given to human dignity owing in large measure to an expanded human rights discourse which began.[52] Newly independent states inserted chapters on human rights into their constitutions and, consequently, referenced human dignity. Notable among the new constitutional provisions which recognized dignity as a constitutional right were Russia, Israel, South Africa, and Germany.[53] Other new constitutions chose, alternatively, to set dignity as a constitutional value.[54] In 1975, the new Greek Constitution acknowledged the importance of human dignity as did Portugal, when both were established as democracies.[55] Post-Franco Spain saw recognition of human dignity in its new constitution of 1978.[56]

In sum, the post–WWII rights that were established should be seen properly as a set of rules delimiting appropriate social, political, and economic relationships between states and their populations.[57] These human rights "held promise for the hundreds of millions of people who lived in colonial dependency."[58] Sadly, these trans-national rights still remain unrealized for many.[59] Yet, since the end of World War II, generic human rights have nonetheless been recognized as norms and as legitimate criteria for not only asserting, establishing, and maintaining political legitimacy,[60] but human rights have now achieved such a universal pre-eminence that a modern state is seen as neither legitimate nor complete without an accounting of a human rights record.[61]

CONTEMPORARY UNDERSTANDINGS: IMPRECISIONS AND PENUMBRAS

Human dignity, quite simply, then, goes to the very heart of what being a person embraces in a value system. Yet, as a theorized concept, dignity has often been seen—as observed—as "incomplete," because, to be an adequate normative account, it lacks a "well-specified counterpart obligation."[62] Even with a "charge" of incompleteness, a fundamental assertion may be made: namely, that there is an overlapping, consensus that exists regarding the values which underlie the acceptance of dignity as a human right where worth must be secured and protected by the states.[63]

Over succeeding years, as in the past, the focus of the "human rights debate" will be the extent to which economic, social, and cultural rights are as cognizable and equal as civil and political rights.[64] Arguments will seek to either prioritize rights—placing differing moral rights on them—or, alternatively, asserting that fundamental rights cannot be ranked, but must be equally honored.[65] The perception of the inferiority of economic, social, and cultural rights to civil and political rights, raises a serious concern that endowing such rights with "human rights status" would have the end result of "weakening traditional human rights" and thus play havoc with the notion of allowing violations of economic, social, and cultural rights to be justiciable.[66]

"A common ground of moral understanding" must be reached before minimum standards of behavior can be negotiated and, ideally, morphed by all states into a standard of universality for the uniform application of human rights.[67] Once a basic acceptance of "performance" standards is attained, adjustments can be allowed—tied as such to differing legal, moral, and cultural value systems within each state.[68] Yet, even with the attainment of this ideal model scenario, where by treaty, acquiesce, or custom states arise to a "universal" acceptance and enforcement of human rights, one overpowering geopolitical policy consideration must be understood: namely, that the core determinants of the level of respect, protection, and enforcement of those rights is tied, unalterably, to the level of economic development and self-sufficiency of each state.[69]

NOTES

1. C. Ben Mitchell, Ch. 3, *The Audacity of The Imago Dei*, at 93 in IMAGO DEI: HUMAN DIGNITY IN ECUMENICAL PERSPECTIVE (Thomas A. Howard ed., 2013). *Imago Dei* invokes characteristics such as "human creativity, the capacity for relationships and community, and responsible compassionate stewardship for others." Courtney Campbell, Ch. 8, *Principlism and Religion: The Law and The Prophets* at 187 in A MATTER OF PRINCIPLES? FERMENT IN U.S. BIOETHICS (Edwin R. DuBose, Ronald P. Namel & Lawrence J. O'Connell eds., 1994).

2. GARY B. FERNGREN, MEDICINE AND HEALTH CARE IN EARLY CHRISTIANITY 95 (2009).

3. Mitchell, *supra* note 1 at 94. *See* Yair Lorberbaum, *Blood and The Image of God: On the Sanctity of Life in Biblical and Early Rabbinic Law, Myth and Ritual* at 55 in CONCEPT OF HUMAN DIGNITY IN HUMAN RIGHTS DISCOURSE [hereinafter CONCEPT OF HUMAN DIGNITY] (David Kretzmer & Eckart Klein eds., 2002). The author observes that *Imago Dei* was not the sole basis for developing the conceptual value of human dignity in Western Cultures—this, because *Imago Dei* was found originally in Mesopotamia and possibly in Ancient Egypt. *Id.* at 55. *See also* James Hanvey, Ch. 11, *Dignity, Person, and Imago Trinitas* at 209 in UNDERSTANDING HUMAN DIGNITY [hereinafter UNDERSTANDING DIGNITY] (Christopher McCrudden ed., 2015) (maintaining that the common route to an understanding is through the idea of *Imago Dei*). *See generally* Doron Shulziner, *A Jew's Conception of Human Dignity* 34 J. RELIGIOUS ETHICS 663 (Dec. 2006).

4. Mitchell, *supra* note 1 at 94–95. *See* David Gelernter, *The Irreducibly Religious Character of Human Dignity*, in HUMAN DIGNITY AND BIOETHICS: ESSAYS COMMISSIONED BY THE PRESIDENT'S COUNCIL ON BIOETHICS 387 (2008).

5. Mitchell, *supra* note 1 at 94. *See* John F. Crosby, *The Twofold Sources of the Divinity of Persons*, 18 FAITH & PHILOSOPHY 292 (July, 2001). *See also* Janet Soskice, Ch. 12, *Human Dignity and The Image of God* in UNDERSTANDING DIGNITY, *supra* note 3.

6. Mitchell, *supra* note 1 at 111. Dignity is defined as the quality of being worthy and honorable, worthiness, worth, nobleness, exclusive, the quality of being worthy of something. IV OX. ENGLISH DICTIONARY 656 (1989).

7. STEPHEN JAMES, UNIVERSAL RIGHTS 8 (2007).

8. *Id.*

9. GEORGE KATEB, HUMAN DIGNITY 13–14 (2013).

10. *Id.* at 13.

11. *Id.*

12. The Roman Catholic tradition acknowledges that "not all dignity is human dignity." Rather, human dignity is but one form of dignity. MICHAEL ROSEN, DIGNITY: ITS HISTORY AND MEANING at 19 (2012).

13. KATEB, *supra* note 9 at 14.

14. *Id.*

15. *Id. But see* ALLEN W. WOOD, KANT'S ETHICAL THOUGHT (1999) (arguing that the ethical vision of Kant is integral to the idea that dignity is but the rational nature of man).

16. KATEB, *supra* note 9 at 14.

17. *See generally* George P. Smith, II, THE CHRISTIAN RELIGION AND BEOTECHNOLOGY: A SEARCH FOR PRINCIPLED DECISIONMAKING (2006).

18. MICHAEL ROSEN, DIGNITY: ITS HISTORY AND MEANING 48 (2012).

19. *Id.* at 49.

20. *See* Christopher McCrudden, *Human Dignity and Judicial Interpretation of Human Rights*, 19 EUROPEAN J. INT'L L. 655, 662 (2008).

21. *See* http://www.papal/encyclicals.net/John_23/j3pacem.htm.

22. McCrudden, *supra* note 20. All of the citations to the papal encyclicals cited may be found at www.papalencycylicals.net/.

23. *On the Christian Meaning of Suffering*, Salvific Doloris, Apostolic Letter, Feb. 11, 1984 at p. 38.

24. *Id.* at 35.

25. *Id.* at 4. *See* George P. Smith, II, *Cura Personalis: A Healthcare Delivery Quandary at The End of Life*, 7 ST. LOUIS U. J. HEALTH L. & POL'Y 311 (2014).

26. *See* http://www.vatican.va/holy_father/benedict_xvi/speeches/2006/march/documents/hf_ben...

27. Junno Arocho Esteves, *Holy Year is a reminder to put mercy before judgment, Pope says, CATHOLIC STANDARD*, Dec. 17, 2015, at 3. *See also* www.dynamiccatholic.com/year-of-mercy. *See also* Robert P. Kraymak, *Human Dignity and the Mystery of the Human Soul*, Ch. 4 in HUMAN DIGNITY AND BIOETHICS, *supra* note 4, President's Council on Bioethics.

28. John Milbank, Ch. 10, *Dignity Rather Than Rights* at 189 in UNDERSTANDING DIGNITY, *supra* note 3.

29. ROSEN, *supra* note 18 at 53.

30. GG Res 217A (III), at UN GAOR, 3d Sess. 1st plen mtg UN Doc A/810 (12 December 1948).

31. 16 December 1966, 933 UNTS 3 (the United States is not a party).

32. 16 December 1966, 999 UNTS 171 (the United States is a party, subject to several reservations, understandings and declarations). Collectively, these three dignitarian instruments are seen as the International Bill of Rights. STEPHEN JAMES, *supra* note 7. *See* PATRICK CAPPS, HUMAN DIGNITY AND THE FOUNDATIONS OF INTERNATIONAL LAW (2009). *See generally* Larry Johnson, *The United Nations System for the Protection of Human Rights*, 20 GA. J. INT'L. & COMP. L. 363 (1990).

33. George P. Smith, II, *Human Rights and Bioethics: Formulating a Universal Right to Health Care or Health Protection?* 38 VANDERBILT J. TRANSNAT'L. L. 1295 (2005).

34. GA Res 217A (III), at UN GAOR, 3d Sess, 1st plen mtg UNDOC A/810 (12 December 1948). *See* Klaus Dicke, *The Founding Function of Human Dignity in the Universal Declaration of Human Rights*, at 111 in THE CONCEPT OF HUMAN DIGNITY at supra note 3.

35. Adam McBeth, *Privatising Human Rights: What Happens to the State's Human Rights Duties When Services are Privatised?* 5 MELBOURNE J. INT'L. L. 133, 143 (2004).

36. *Id.* Today, many human rights no longer limit state powers, alone, but have been privatized, HOLGER HESTERMEYER, HUMAN RIGHTS AND THE WTO (2007).

37. Gerard Brennan, *Foreword*, in CONSTITUTIONAL ADVANCEMENT IN A FROZEN CONTINENT at viii (H. P. Lee & P. Gerangelos eds., 2009).

38. THERESE MURPHY, HEALTH AND HUMAN RIGHTS 25 (2013).

39. *Id.* at 17.

40. Dicke, *supra* note 34. The Declaration refers to dignity in five places; twice in the Preamble, in Art. 1 and twice in the contexts of social and economic rights in Art. 22 Art. 23, Art. 23, para. 3. Dicke, id. at 114.

41. Yehoshua Arieli, *On the Necessary and Sufficient Conditions for the Emergence of the Doctrine of the Dignity of Man and His Rights* at 5 in CONCEPT OF HUMAN DIGNITY, *supra* note 3. *See generally* Seth Mohney, *The Great Power Origins of Human Rights*, 35 MICH. J. INT'L. L. 828 (2014).

42. Hubert Canick, *'Dignity of Man' and 'Persona'* in *Stoic Anthropology: Some Remarks in Cicero's, De Officiis* in CONCEPT OF HUMAN DIGNITY, *supra* note 3 at 18, 27; Arthur Chaskalson, *Human Dignity as a Constitutional Value* in CONCEPT OF HUMAN DIGNITY, *supra* note 3 at 133.

43. Arieli, *supra* note 41.

44. *Id.*

45. *Id.*

46. *Id.*

47. David Weisstub, *Honor, Dignity, and The Framing of Multicultural Values* in CONCEPT OF HUMAN DIGNITY, *supra* note 3 at 263, 274.

48. *Id.*

49. AHARON BARAK, HUMAN DIGNITY: THE CONSTITUTIONAL VALUE AND THE CONSTITUTIONAL RIGHT 40 (2015).

50. *Id.* at 50.

51. *Id.*

52. *Id.* at 51. *See* Doron Shulziner, *Human Dignity in Judicial Decisions: Principles of Application and the Rule of Law*, 23 CARDOZO J. INT'L & COMP. L. 435 (2017); BARAK, *supra* note 49, at 53.

53. *Id.*

54. *Id.*

55. *Id.* at 55.

56. *Id. See* CATHERINE DUPREE, THE AGE OF DIGNITY: HUMAN RIGHTS AND CONSTITUTIONALISM (2015).

57. CHRISTOPHER N. J. ROBERTS, THE CONTENTIOUS HISTORY OF THE INTERNATIONAL BILL OF HUMAN RIGHTS 122 (2015).

58. *Id.* at 123.

59. *See* Rhoda E. Howard & Jack Donnelly, *Human Dignity, Human Rights, and Political Regimes*, 80 AM. POLITICAL SCIENCE REV. 801 (1986).

60. Dr. Eric Heinze, *Even-Handedness and The Politics of Human Rights*, 21 HARV. HUMAN RIGHTS J. 7, 7 (2008). *See* Mohney, *supra* note 41. *See also* DENNIS DAVIS et al., AN ENQUIRY INTO THE EXISTENCE OF GLOBAL VALUES THROUGH THE LAWS OF COMPARATIVE CONSTITUTIONAL LAW (2017).

61. Heinze, *id. See* Carrie Booth Walling, *Human Rights Norms, State Sovereignty, and Humanitarian Interventions*, 37 HUM. RTS. Q. 383 (2015) (analyzing the changing meanings of state sovereignty to legitimize and protect human rights norms). *See also* Stephen P. Marlos, *Normative Expansion of The Right To Health and The Proliferation of Human Rights*, 49 GEO. WASH. INT'L. L. REV. 97 (2016).

62. JOHN TOBIN, THE RIGHT TO HEALTH IN INTERNATIONAL LAW 11 (2012).

63. *Id.* at 375. *See* JONATHAN HERRING, CARING AND THE LAW, Ch. 4 (2013) (stressing the obligation of the state to support care and promote Social Justice). *See also* George P. Smith, II, *Justice and Health Care Management: An Elusive Quest*, 9 HOUS. J. HEALTH LAW & POL'Y 1 (2009).

64. HESTERMEYER, *supra* note 36 at 93.

65. *Id.*

66. *Id. See* LOCAL ENGAGEMENT WITH INTERNATIONAL ECONOMIC LAW AND HUMAN RIGHTS (Ljiljana Biukovic & Pitman B. Potter eds., 2017).

67. Belinda J. Bennett, *Globalization Rights? Constructing Health Rights in a Shrinking World*, Ch. 1 at 20 in BRAVE NEW WORLD OF HEALTH (Belinda J. Bennett, Tim Carney & Ilizabeth Karpin eds., 2008). *See* HUMAN RIGHTS IN GLOBAL HEALTH: RIGHTS-BASED GOVERNANCE FOR A GLOBALIZING WORLD (Benjamin M. Meier & Lawrence O. Gostin eds., 2018) for a comprehensive analysis of the evolution of human rights into the architecture of global health.

See generally Michael J. Perry, *The Morality of Human Rights*, 50 SAN DIEGO L. REV. 775 (2013).

68. *See generally* George P. Smith, II, HUMAN RIGHTS AND BIOMEDICINE (2000). *See also* Leonard Hoffman, *The Universality of Human Rights*, 125 L. Q. REV. 416 (2009).

69. *See* Andrew K. Woods, *A Behavioral Approach to Human Rights*, 51 HARV. INT'L. L. J. 51, 70 (2010). *See also* WALTER KÄLIN & JÖRG KÜNZLI, THE LAW OF INTERNATIONAL RIGHTS PROTECTION at 319 (2004).

Chapter 3

The Indignities of Pain and of Suffering at the End-of-Life

Founded in 1973, the International Association for the Study of Pain's principal focus is to promote the development of national policies regarding the management of pain as a health problem.[1] In the Declaration of Montreal put forward by the Association in October, 2010, the European Federation for Pain Study—and led by the World Health Organization—several propositions were advanced: namely, that withholding pain treatment is wrong and leads to unnecessary suffering, which is harmful; that there is a right of all people to have access to pain management without discrimination; and that failure to establish policies, practices, and systems which offer pain management is unethical and "in breach of the patient's human rights."[2]

CHRONIC PAIN

Recognizing that the physical and psychosocial etiology of chronic pain sufferers manifests itself through a variety of conditions, including depression, anxiety, fear, and even suicide,[3] these three organizations defined chronic pain as pain recurring for a period of more than three months.[4] The broad nature of this definition finds support in both European and American studies. Not only do these studies disclose the significant employment irregularities resulting from chronic pain sufferers,[5] but surveys of households in Europe and the United States revealed that 36 percent of Europeans may be classified as chronic pain sufferers, and in America, 43 percent of all households had members in chronic pain.[6] That percentage for Americans translates into a raw figure of eight million. By 2030, this figure is expected to double.[7]

Within this demographic is another projection that, if accurate, presages even greater stress on health care resources for the elderly and underscores the ultimate need for a system attuned to the needs of long-term end-of-life care. If, indeed, the over-65 population in the United States will rise more than 70 percent between 2010 and 2030, while payroll taxes for those within the general population rise, as predicted, less than 4 percent, it is clear that planning efforts must be under taken presently in order to meet these systematic needs.[8]

Several organizations have made attempts to plan for the needs of end-of-life patients. The WHO has developed a three-step "ladder" for cancer pain relief. In summary, it states:

> If pain occurs, there should be prompt oral administration of drugs in the following order: Non-opioids (aspirin and paracetamol); then strong opioids such as morphine, until the patient is free of pain. To calm fears and anxiety, additional drugs—"adjuvants"—should be used. To maintain freedom from pain, drugs should be given "by the clock," that is every 3–6 hours, rather than "on demand." This three-step approach of administering the right drug in the right dose at the right time is inexpensive and 80–90% effective. Surgical intervention on appropriate nerves may provide further pain relief if drugs are not wholly effective.[9]

The President's Council on Bioethics concluded in 2005 that the basic standard for clinical decision-making should be one that promotes the best patient care.[10] This standard obviously must be continually adjusted as a patient's case history progresses,[11] and to promote patient care anchored in mercy, compassion, beneficence, and loving charity—care which recognizes that relief of pain is the most universal moral obligation that a physician must uphold and that there is, indeed, a right not to suffer.[12]

Psychological distress, or existential pain, however, is usually difficult to assess because evaluation requires special training and continual contact with the patients' families.[13] There is a general societal aversion to the obstacles faced in proving a patient's emotional distress at end-of-life care.[14] Distinguishing between depression and psychological morbidity is difficult because the sympathology of disrupted sleeping patterns, loss of energy, and lack of appetite are not exclusive response mechanisms to psychological distress, but appear in cancer and other terminal illnesses as well.[15] Because of these difficulties and uncertainties, the palliative management of existential pain has been largely neglected.[16]

While no general "solutions" exist for meeting the existential needs of terminally ill patients, attempts to meet these needs require careful listening skills and defined lines of communication between health care providers, patients, affected families, and proxy or surrogate decision-makers. Valid existential concerns are often obscured during palliative care treatment.[17] Even though a patient may have no absolute control over the wide and varied spectra of suffering, the patient still has freedom to choose what attitude is taken toward that suffering.[18] By extending end-of-life care to include psychiatric, psychological, existential, and spiritual issues—consistent with the WHO's definition of palliative care and its goal of addressing total patient needs[19]—a more complete, compassionate, and realistic approach to managing terminal illness and end-stage suffering would be implemented.[20]

ASSESSING EXISTENTIAL SUFFERING

The desire to hasten death arises because of a number of conditions: inadequate pain management, psychological conditions ranging from depression and hopelessness, to fears to loss of autonomy and physical functioning,[21] to futile and unbearable suffering, and avoidance of humiliation.[22] All of these conditions conduce to one overriding fear: loss of human dignity,[23] which brings with it a fear of being forced to become but a "passive bystander" to all of the normal functions of life.[24] By managing the dying process, which, for some, is viewed as too protracted and filled with growing and multiple functional losses,[25] the patient can exert some level of control over a process that is acknowledged to be "by and large, a messy business."[26] Sadly, this complicated and vexatious process for implementing the "new epidemiology of dying"[27] almost assures that health care providers will follow heroic procedures which do *not* promote or sustain quality so much as postpone death.[28]

In approximately 25 percent of all terminally ill patients, depression and other mood disorders occur.[29] Yet, interestingly, few receive pharmacological aid through anti-depressant prescriptions.[30] As this book shows, the main obstacle to a more liberal response to these patients' needs is the lack of clarity in determining when a distressed, terminal patient is suffering from clinical depression or, instead, exhibiting a "normal grief response" to the dying process.[31] The components of both of these syndromes are often vague, imprecise, and difficult to evaluate.[32] Commonly, when patients are obsessed with feelings of worthlessness, lose their ability and desire to interact socially, and, indeed, lose their sense of hope, they are properly assessed as suffering from clinical depression[33] and should be given whatever dosage of analgesic is deemed necessary to alleviate that condition—this, because pharmacotherapy is ultimately the principal tool for symptom control.[34]

Another drawback to accurate and prompt evaluations of psychological distress or existential suffering is often the inability of a physician or palliative care management team to understand patient views about suffering. As a spiritual phenomenon, suffering is often accepted in Christian communities as a meaningful and authentic community response to Jesus Christ's own suffering.[35] In some faith communities, cultural efforts are expended in order to view suffering—physically and mentally—as a positive, reinforcing value.[36] Merely accepting suffering as authentic, however, does not mean that it is also meaningful.[37] It remains for the physician to ascertain and then listen carefully to the spiritual parameters within each patient's character[38] in an attempt to treat those seriously ill as "whole persons."[39] In this way, the therapy is truly patient-centered.[40]

Refractory existential suffering—or those symptoms that defy adequate control despite all efforts to provide relief—is difficult to distinguish during the end stages of life from physical distress.[41] Those additional refractory symptoms most commonly reported as requiring palliative sedation are: various degrees of agitation, restlessness or distress, confusion, respiratory distress, pain, and myoclonus (e.g., severe twitching, jerking, or uncontrollable shakes).[42]

Palliative sedation therapy is thus defined as "the use of sedative medications to relieve intolerable and refractory distress by the reduction in patient consciousness."[43] When patient suffering—physical or existential—becomes refractory to standard palliative therapies, the human, compassionate, and merciful response is to offer terminal sedation.[44] This approach to medical treatment may be seen as consistent with sound principles of adjusted care.

Demoralization

It has been suggested that—in the clinical setting of hospice or palliative care—a unique diagnostic category, termed the "demoralization syndrome," is becoming more recognizable and should be refined and classified as a cognitive disorder.[45] Seen as a "useful category of existential distress in which meaningless predominates and . . . profound hopelessness and [a] desire to die may result,"[46] this syndrome, if not treated satisfactorily with pharmacological therapy, should render such a demoralized patient incompetent to make medical decisions.[47]

Yet, interestingly, there is no conclusive empirical evidence to support an all-too-popular conclusion that depression so impairs judgment as to prevent one from competently disapproving of the initiation or cessation of medical treatment.[48] Sadly, this depression argument would appear to be a ruse to obstruct and even prevent end-of-life decision-making on the grounds of moral repugnancy to alternative or surrogate health care providers.[49]

If, and when, the demoralization syndrome is accepted by diagnosticians as a cognitive disorder, it would then remain for physicians to respond with compassion and caring in remediating this medical condition. If deemed proper, under the overarching principle of medical futility, physicians should consider the reasonableness of alleviating this pathological mental state in the end-stage patient by administering terminal sedation. Such a course of treatment would be consistent with the central obligation of all physicians to alleviate pain and suffering—here, mental suffering and/or "existential helplessness"[50]—in order to assure the dying patient's dignity and best interests.[51]

THE PROCESS OF DYING

Judicial Guidance

For purposes of this chapter, and the issue of end-of-life care, the concurrence for Justice Sandra Day O'Connor in the 1989 case of *Cruzan v. Director, Missouri Dept. of Health, et al.*, is pertinent.[52]

Holding that the refusal of food and water delivered artificially was to be viewed as an act within a protected liberty interest and properly refused as unwanted medical treatment, Justice O'Connor observed that "our notions of liberty are inextricably entwined with an idea of physical freedom and self-determination," and, furthermore, a state that forces "a competent adult to endure such procedures against her will burdens the patient's liberty, dignity, and freedom to determine the course of her own treatment."[53] Stressing the compromise of the "integrity of personhood" by forcible intrusions of this nature, the Justice asserted that "the liberty guaranteed by the Due Process Clause must protect, if it protects anything, an individual's deeply personal decision to reject medical treatment including the artificial delivery of good and water."[54] The very same "minimal conditions necessary for a life in dignity,"[55] then (e.g., autonomy, respect, self-determination, compassion, humaneness, decency) are the very same conditions and values which should prevail in the management of the end-stage of life.

The *Cruzan* case was pivotal in developing a constitutional jurisprudence for end-of-life management. The notion of a recognized liberty interest in dying without refractory pain and suffering—both for competent and incompetent patients[56]—was validated by the *Cruzan* holding.[57] As a consequence of this liberty interest in dying without pain, with as much dignity as possible, when challenges to its exercise are raised, courts would proceed to balance this liberty against competing state interests to protect vulnerables (e.g., the aged and infirm unhealthy).[58] State interest in preserving a terminally ill person's life would obviously be weaker than preserving life that is not in its terminal phase.[59] The *Cruzan* construct for decision-making—anchored, as such, in the Common Law right to refuse treatment—is a more reasonable approach to analysis than validating a fundamental right to die with dignity.[60]

Were a right to death be recognized as a fundamental right, a vexatious dilemma would follow: namely, whether the state would be charged, correspondingly, with an equal obligation to both bestow, as well as guarantee, a life with dignity?[61] "If enduring dignity at death is the responsibility, dignity during life is an equal, if not greater, responsibility."[62] Under circumstances of this nature, it would follow that dignity would be denominated an entitlement.[63] Although set as a responsibility within modern state institutions,[64] dignity in life is not a precise and integral value in the U.S. Constitution.[65] It is better to view the Constitution as providing negative rights rather than affirmative ones.[66] Consequently, citizens are granted liberty to access—without government power—their individual consciences and visions for attaining happiness.[67] The relationship between the U.S. Constitution and death is difficult for courts to determine.[68] The legislatures are far better equipped to enact statutes which draw lines of distinction for example, between physicians assisted suicide and euthanasia.[69]

When presented with issues of physician assisted suicide and the states' right to prohibit it, the Supreme Court has held in two pathbreaking cases—*Vaco v. Quill*[70] and in *Washington v. Glucksberg*[71]—that it was valid, constitutionally, to prohibit suicide—especially since the idea of physician assisted suicide was neither a part of the Nation's history nor its traditions;[72] and laws prohibiting such conduct were not in contravention of the Equal Protection Clause of the 14th Amendment.[73]

In the concurring opinions in both *Quill* and *Glucksberg*, Justice O'Connor implies that a constitutional liberty exists, when a terminal medical condition is diagnosed, to be free from the refractory pain experienced from such a condition.[74] But, without "great suffering," there can be no constitutional claim.[75] In these two cases, there was adequate pain relief available legally to the moving parties.[76] Accordingly, the "liberty" found in the Due Process Clause—which could arguably embrace a coordinate liberty to use assistance in an out of suicide, motivated solely to avoid a painful and undignified death—was not an "operable" fact in these cases.[77] There was a direct implication, however, in Justice O'Connor's concurrence that in situations where no intractable pain was present and no state legislation was in play, a different judicial result might result.[78]

Justice John Paul Stevens, in his concurrence in *Glucksberg*, recognizes Justice O'Connor's notion of a liberty interest as central to any action to avoid intolerable pain "and the indignity of living one's final days incapacitated and in agony."[79] When statutory mandates are either vague and indeterminate or lacking altogether, this formulation should be seen as more judicially palpable than seeking precise limits to a "right" to die with dignity.[80]

In 1992, the case of *Planned Parenthood v. Casey* held that the state of Pennsylvania was allowed to regulate abortion in the first trimester, or at any point of viability and beyond, so long as their regulations did not pose an undue burden on a woman's right to abortion.[81] Justice Anthony Kennedy, in a plurality opinion with Justices O'Connor and Souter, observed eloquently:

> … matters involving the most intimate and personal choices a person may make in a lifetime, choices central to personal dignity and autonomy, are central to the liberty protected by the Fourteenth Amendment. At the heart of liberty is the right to define one's own concept of existence, of meaning, of themselves, and of the mystery of human life.[82]

It is obvious, then, that under both *Cruzan*[83] and *Casey*,[84] and based upon notions of self-determination, personal choice, and autonomy, legal grounds for a right to assistance in suicide or in euthanasia are established.[85]

Respecting the personal autonomy of its citizens, the state must foreswear any effort to promote particular moral objectives or ends.[86] Individuals must be given freedom to choose any life values they desire—which certainly might well include the wish to end their life with or without assistance.[87] This freedom of action or self-control is to be restricted only when it threatens or becomes a harm to others.[88] In the final analysis, the single most significant criterion for assisting dying should be an assessment of personal suffering and not the nature of an individual illness.[89] For a disabled person, living in a chronic condition of refractory pain and suffering, death could well be a "salvation."[90]

Elaborating upon the vitality of the freedom of choice, others have suggested that—using a utilitarian calculus—the legalization of assistance at death would be efficient because the benefits associated with legalization (safeguarding autonomy and liberty) outweigh attendant costs.[91] Richard Epstein would, while following the libertarian ideal of self-determination, limit this right of assisted suicide and euthanasia to the terminally ill and those with unremitting suffering.[92]

More contemporaneously, on June 26, 2015, writing for the majority in *Obergefell et al., v. Hodges et al.*,[93] Justice Anthony M. Kennedy articulated repeatedly the need to acknowledge and to embrace the realization that "certain personal choices [are] central to individual dignity and autonomy" and are inherent liberties protected by Due Process guarantees of the 14th Amendment.[94] While these expanded liberties are, as such, not enumerated within the Bill of Rights, they must nevertheless be accepted as within the "concept of individual autonomy."[95] When "a claim of dignity" conflicts "with both law and widespread social conventions," as well as "substantial cultural and political developments,"[96] the conflicts must be resolved in favor of safeguarding the dignity of personhood.[97] By way of analogy, Justice Kennedy's positions in *Obergefell*[98] clearly illustrate that the dignity of personhood is as important in its formation as it is in health care decision-making at the end-stage of life where personal autonomy and wellbeing, humanness, and compassion are vital components to assure a dignified death.

Legislative Responses

Legislatively, five states and the District of Columbia have enacted laws that allow those with a terminal medical condition to seek pharmacologic assistance from a physician to end their own lives.[99] One state supreme court, Montana, concluded that while there was no constitutional right to die with dignity in the state, physician assistance for those in the end-stage of life was not violative of state legislation designed to protect the terminally ill, nor was such assistance against state public policy to protect vulnerable individuals.[100] Similarly, in parts of Europe—notably, the Netherlands, Belgium, and Switzerland—a legislative right of the terminally ill to have assistance in ending their lives has been recognized.[101]

Caring Responses in a Just Society

In contemporary society, it has been urged that sympathy and compassion must be integrated into the fabric of the law.[102] A modern and principled rule of law, then, needs notions of decency and compassion within its sinews[103] and does not have to conflict with a rule of love.[104] Others have called for the law to be empathetic, a term often used interchangeably with love, altruism, and sympathy.[105]

One of the inherent weaknesses of the rule of law has been said to be its all too often efforts to distance itself from human experience.[106] A strong claim could be made that introducing human values or attitudes into the judicial process would conflict with the idea of judgment sustained by rational and objective argumentation, not feelings and emotions.[107] Thus, empathetic discourse runs the risk of being seen as irrelevant and dismissed.[108]

Whether health care policies be legislative, judicial, or medical, there should be one operable normative standard for guidance and for action.[109] Termed agape, charity, compassion, love, or mercy, this common unifying denominator in palliative care is a humane, morally responsible approach to maintaining dignity at the end-stage of life when faced with refractory pain and intractable suffering.[110]

Judicial decision-makers, just as health care providers, must exercise good judgment. Good judgment is characterized as "an elusive . . . compound of *empathy*, modesty, maturity, a sense of proportion, balance, a recognition of human limitations, sanity, prudence, a sense of reality and *common sense*.[111] This elusive trait must be the norm when making medicolegal decisions, not the exception.

It has been argued persuasively that while the state may declare a legitimate interest in morality,[112] it cannot easily sacrifice "claims of associational autonomy"[113] found in "expressive [or] intimate association"[114] in order to protect public morality. Accordingly, care must be taken by the state to eschew administrative, judicial, or legislative determinations that abridge "choices central to personal dignity and autonomy . . . central to the liberty protected by the Fourteenth Amendment."[115]

It is logical to assume that the right to compassionate care in end-stage illness is grounded in a liberty interest and cannot be unduly challenged or restricted by a state interest in judging the "morality" of autonomous actions designed to give purpose and promote dignity.[116] Society's central obligation is not to mandate one moral code over another but rather, to define and safeguard "the liberty of all"[117] and promote social policies which address suffering with charity, compassion, and common sense.[118] Inextricable to this societal obligation is recognition of a coordinate duty of health care providers "not to prolong dying."[119] This duty arguably coalesces with, and validates, the very principle of beneficence,[120] and thereby shapes a new "right" of the terminally ill to be free from refractory pain and existential suffering at the end-stage of life.[121]

The ever-present fear of forcing society onto a slippery slope that ends in the unequivocal endorsement and unrestricted practice of active euthanasia should not serve as an excuse for passivity or ineptitude in the formulation of public policy and in decision making.[122] Rather, contemporary standards of normative conduct grounded in simple notions of compassionate dignity, beneficence, love, mercy, or charity should prevail as the foundations for end-of-life decision making. Ideally, this conduct will lead to the simple recognition of a human right to avoid intractable somatic or non-somatic pain and suffering.[123] Individuals must have a right to be free from the cruel and unusual punishment[124] of being forced to live despite being diagnosed as being in a futile medical condition.[125]

In reality, the slippery slope is nothing more than the inescapable human condition.[126] The common duty of man is but to "struggle along" in reaching a common destiny—a life struggle which is either "upwards or downwards, with very uncertain footing."[127] No safe plateau of moral security can ever be reached in the journey of life.[128] Rather, painful dilemmas of choice are the rule rather than the exception. Perhaps, in reality, the "goal of the human moral effort" should be simply "to keep seeing and drawing the line, and struggling to stay above it."[129]

NOTES

1. *See* http://www.iasp-painorg/AboutIASP/.
2. *Id.*
3. Arthur G. Lipman, *Pain as a Human Right: The 2004 Global Day Against Pain*, 19 J. Pain & Palliative Care Pharmacotherapy 85, 86 (2005).
4. *Id.* at 88.
5. *Id.* at 89.
6. *Id.* at 88.
7. Bruce Jenner et al., *Access to Hospice Care: Expanding Boundaries, Overcoming Boundaries*, 33 HASTINGS CENTER REP. at S1 (March–April 2003).
8. *Id.* It is estimated that in order to support Medicare and Medicaid program costs, payroll taxes must rise 4 percent. *Id.*
9. *WHO's Pain Ladder*, WORLD HEALTH ORG., http://www/who.int.cancer/palliative/painladder/en/index.html (last visited Nov. 8, 2017).
10. President's Council on Bioethics, Taking Care: Ethical Caregiving in Our Aging Society 217 (2005), *available at* http://bioethics.georgetown.edu/pcbe/reports/taking_care/. Best patient care is adjusted to the developing medical needs of the patient. Essential to the standard of best care is acceptance of the "intrinsic dignity of persons" which, in turn, mandates that the goal of providing care must be to enhance total patient well-being (somatic and non-somatic) and, at the end of life, demonstrate beneficence, compassion, or charity in managing pain and suffering. David C. Thomasma, Human Life in the Balance 165, 184 (1990). *See* Edmund D. Pellegrino & David C. Thomasma, For the Patient's Own Good: The Restoration of Beneficence in Health Care (1988). *See also* David C. Thomasma & Glenn C. Graber, Euthanasia: Toward an Ethical Social Policy 192 (1991) for a discussion of the principle of adjusted care.
11. Thomasma & Graeber, *id.* at 129.
12. *Id.* at 192, 194 (quoting Dr. Edmund D. Pellegrino). *But see* Kelly Dineen & James DuBois, *Between a Rock and a Hard Place: Can Physicians Prescribe Opioids to Treat Pain Adequately While Avoiding Legal Sanction?* 41 Am. J. L. & Med. 53 (2016).
13. Manish Agrawal & Ezekial J. Emanuel, *Attending to Psychologic Symptoms and Palliative Care*, 20 J. Clinical Oncology 624 (Feb. 1, 2001); ROB BODDICE, PAIN (2017).
14. *Id.*; *see generally* Paul Arnstein et al., *Self Efficacy as a Mediator of the Relationship between Pain Intensity, Disability and Depression in Chronic Pain Patients*, 80 Pain 483 (1999) (calling for further research after conducting a study which showed a possible connection between chronic pain and low self-efficacy—doubts about one's own abilities).

15. Put simply, the dying "do not have the luxury of clearly separating their physical suffering from their psychological, spiritual, and existential suffering." Timothy E. Quill & Margaret P. Battin, *Excellent Palliative Care as The Standard, Physician Assisted Dying as a Last Resort* at 323 in PHYSICIAN-ASSISTED DYING: THE CASE FOR PALLIATIVE CARE (Timothy E. Quill & Margaret P. Battin eds., 2004).

16. Agrawal & Emanuel, *supra* note 13. Existential suffering can be as much torture as physical pain. When the limits of suffering are reached, it is natural to view suicide—as Goethe suggests—as a "natural act." *See* JOHANN W. von GOETHE, THE SORROWS OF YOUNG WERTHER, BOOK ONE: LETTERS OF JULY 30–SEPTEMBER 10 (1774) at http://www.gradeserver.com/the-sorrows-of-the-young-werther#. *See also*, ANDRZEJ SZCZEKLIK, CATHARSIS: ON THE ART OF MAN, Ch. VIII, (2005).

17. Ingrid Bolmsjö, et al., *Meeting Existential Needs in Palliative Care—Who, When, and Why?* 18 J. Palliative Care 195 (2002). *See* RICHARD F. GROVES & HENRIETTE A. KLAUSER, THE AMERICAN BOOK OF LIVING AND DYING: LESSONS IN HEALING SPIRITUAL PAIN (2009); SZCZEKLIK, *id.*

18. William Breitbart, Christopher Gibson, Shannon Poppito & Amy Berg, *Psychotherapeutic Interventions at the End of Life: A Focus on Meaning and Spirituality*, 49 Can. J. Psychiatry 336 (June, 2004). *See also* George P. Smith, II, Final Choices: Autonomy in Health Care Decisions (1989).

19. Hospice: The Living Idea (Cicely Saunders et al. eds., 1981); Hospice Care on The International Scene at 320 (Cicely Saunders & Robert Kastenbaum eds., 1997). *See generally*, Sam Halabi, *Selling Hospice* 42 J. L. MED. & ETHICS 442 (2014).

20. Breitbart et al., *supra* note 18, at 371.

21. Helene Stacks et al., *Why Now? Timing and Circumstances of Hastened Deaths*, 30 J. Pain & Symptom MGMT. 215, 225 (2005).

22. Gerrit Van der Wal & Robert J. M. Dillman, *Euthanasia in the Netherlands*, 308 Br. Med. J. 1346 (1994). *See* Cynthia Bumgardner, *Euthanasia and Assisted Suicide in the United States and The Netherlands*, 10 INDIANA INT'L & COMPARATIVE L. REV. 387 (2000).

23. DEREK HUMPHRY, FINAL EXIT at 135–36 (2010). *See* SZCZEKLIK, *supra* note 16.

24. Richard B. Gunderman, *Is Suffering the Enemy*? 32 Hastings CTR. REP. 40, 43 (2002).

25. Stacks et al., *supra* note 21 at 216.

26. Sherwin B. Nuland, How We Die: Reflections on Life's Final Chapter 142 (1994). *See* Randi R. Oster, *Doctors Should Hear Our Dying Wishes*, WASH. POST, April 28, 2018 at A17.

27. *Id.* at 12.

28. JOANNE LYNN, Sick To Death and Not Going To Take it Anymore! at 164–65 (2004).

29. Karel E. Miller, Stephen M. Adams & Martha M. Miller, *Antidepressant Medication Use in Palliative Care*, 23 AM. J. Hospice & Palliative Med. 127 (No. 2, Mar.–Apr. 2006). Fatal or terminal illnesses often induce grief which is seen

commonly as having five stages: "Denial, Anger, Bargaining, Depression, and Acceptance." PAUL KALANITHI, WHEN BREATH BECOMES AIR 161 (2016).

30. Miller et al., *id.* Some other earlier studies have, however, shown that a number of terminally ill cancer patients have, indeed, received sedation for psychological or mental agonies. Tatsuya Morita et al., *Terminal Sedation for Existential Distress*, 17 Am. J. Hospice and Palliative Care 189, nn. 4, 6–8 (2000). A 1996 study done of experts on sedation in the U.K. and America found that in 22 percent of cases evaluated, sedation was administered because of patient "anguish" and in 16 percent of cases, it was undertaken because of the "emotional, psychological [or] spiritual distress" of those patients. Susan Chater et al., *Sedation for Intractable Distress in the Dying—A Survey of Experts*, 12 Palliative Med. 255 (1998).

31. Miller et al., *supra* note 29.

32. *Id.*

33. *Id.* at 128.

34. Arthur G. Lipman, *The Scream of Edward Munch: A Profound Portrayal of Existential Pain*, 19 J. Pain & Palliative Care Pharmacotherapy 1, 1–2 (2005). *See* Dineen & DuBois, *supra* note 12.

35. Stan Van Hooft, *The Meanings of Suffering*, 28 Hastings Ctr. Rep. 13 (1998). *See* Stanley HauErwas, God, Medicine, and Suffering, chs. II, III (1990). S*ee also* Groves & Klauser, *supra* note 17.

36. Van Hooft, *id.* at 14.

37. *Id.* at 15.

38. *See* Seth M. Holmes et al., *Screening the Soul: Communication Regarding Spiritual Concerns Among Primary Care Physicians and Seriously Ill Patients Approaching the End of Life*, 23 Am. J. Hospice & Palliative Med. 25, 30 (2006).

39. Alton Hart, Jr. et al., *Hospice Patients' Attitudes Regarding Spiritual Discussion with their Doctors*, 20 Am. J. Hosp. Palliative Care 135 (2003).

40. Holmes, et al., *supra* note 38. *See generally* Alan B. Astrow et al., *Is Failure to Meet Spiritual Needs Associated with Cancer Patients' Perceptions of Quality of Care and their Satisfaction with Care?* 25 J. CLIN. ONCOL. 5753 (2007); Groves & Klauser, *supra* note 17.

41. Paul Rousseau, *Existential Suffering and Palliative Sedation: A Brief Commentary with a Proposal for Clinical Guidelines*, 18 Am. J. Hospice & Palliative care 151 (2001). *See* James Halenbeck, *Terminal Sedation for Intractable Distress: Not Slow Euthanasia but a Prompt Response to Suffering*, 171 Western J. Med. 222 (Oct. 1999).

42. Bernard Lo & Gordon Rubenfeld, *Palliative Sedation in Dying Patients: "We Turn to It When Everything Else Hasn't Worked,"* 294 J.A.M.A. 1810, 1811 (2005); *see generally* Joseph W. Shega et al., *Patients Dying with Dementia: Experience at the End of Life and Impact on Hospice Care*, 35 J. Pain Symptom Mgmt. 499 (2008) (conducting a study that showed patients with dementia who enroll in hospice programs may experience better end-of-life care, though certain "non-treatable" symptoms still persist and cause the majority of distress for patients).

43. Tatsuya Morita et al., *Definition of Sedation for Symptom Relief: A Systematic Literature Review and a Proposal for Operational Criteria*, 24 J. Pain Symptom Mgmt. 447 (2002).

44. Rousseau, *supra* note 41; P. C. Rousseau, *Dying and Terminal Sedation*, 7 Clin. Geriatrics 19, 19 (1999). *See* George P. Smith, II, *Terminal Sedation as Palliative Care: Revalidating a Right to a Good Death*, 7 CAMBRIDGE Q. HEALTHCARE 382 (1989).

45. David W. Kissane, *The Contribution of Demoralization to End of Life Decisionmaking*, 34 Hastings Ctr. Rep. 21, 24 (2004).

46. *Id.* at 23. While anxiety and depression are viewed as "expressions of morality"—thereby making them "synonymous with suffering (and) existential distress," demoralization may occur "independently of depression." *Id.* at 23, 24.

47. Kissane, *supra* note 45 at 29.

48. Ronald A. Lindsay, Future Bioethics: Overcoming Taboos, Myths and Dogmas 111 (2008).

49. *Id.* at 112.

50. J. M. BerNstein, Torture and Dignity: An Essay on Moral Injury 177 (2015).

51. *See* Thomasma & Graber, *supra* note 10, at 192, 194 (quoting Dr. Edmund D. Pellegrino). All too often those suffering with dementia in the end-stage of life receive an array of aggressive therapies from forced tube feeding to hospitalization for pneumonia—all of which are not only of limited benefit but inconsistent with sound standards of palliative management.

52. 497 U.S. 261, at 287–89 (1989) (O'Connor, J. concurring).

53. 497 U.S. 261, at 287. *See* Jane E. Brody, *To Hasten the End, Some Patients Don't Eat or Drink*, N.Y. Times, October 25, 2016 at D5 (where policies for voluntarily stopping eating and drinking—VSED—are discussed and where it is observed that death by dehydration usually comes within 7 to 14 days and that adequate pain medication be administered during this process). *See* B. White et al., *Voluntary Palliated Starvation: A Lawful and Ethical Way to Die?* 22 J. LAW & MED. 376 (2014).

54. 497 U.S. at 287.

55. 497 U.S. at 289. *See* WALTER KÄLIN & JORG KÜNZLI, THE LAW OF INTERNATIONAL HUMAN RIGHTS 303 (2004). *See* Jordan J. Paust, *The Human Right to Die with Dignity: A Policy Oriented Essay*, 17 HUM. RIGHTS Q. 463 (1995).

56. While a majority of the Court appeared to assume that a right to refuse life-sustaining treatment survived incompetency, the Rehnquist "official" majority would limit its holding only to competent patients. FOLEY, *infra* note 58 at 185.

57. 497 U.S. 261 (1989).

58. ELIZABETH FOLEY, THE LAW OF LIFE AND DEATH, 184–85 (2011).

59. *Id.* at 184.

60. *Id.* at 184.

61. *Id.* at 183.

62. *Id.* at 183–84.

63. FOLEY, *supra* note 58 at 184.

64. *Id.*

65. *Id.*

66. *Id.*

67. *Id.* at 184, 199.

68. *Id.* at 180, 184, 199. *See* Symposium, *Exploring the Right to Die*, 33 GA. ST. U.L. REV. 869 (2017).

69. FOLEY, *supra* note 58 at 177. Symposium, *id. See* L. W. SUMNER, PHYSICIAN-ASSISTED DEATH: WHAT EVERYONE NEEDS TO KNOW, Chs. 3, 7, 10 (2017).

70. 521 U.S. 793 (1997).

71. 521 U.S. 702 (1997).

72. FOLEY, *supra* note 58 at 177.

73. *Id. See generally* George P. Smith, II, *Refractory Pain, Existential Suffering and Palliative Care: Releasing an Unbearable Lightness of Being*, 20 CORNELL J. L. & PUB. POLICY 469 (2011) (analyzing the extent to which the state should act to establish and then implement a human right to avoid refractory pain and existential suffering in end-state illness). *See also*, DAVID NAGEL, NEEDLESS SUFFERING: HOW SOCIETY FAILS THOSE WITH CHRONIC PAIN (2016).

74. *Id.* at 180.

75. FOLEY, *supra* note 58 at 179.

76. *Id.*

77. *Id.*

78. *Id.*

79. 521 U.S. at 745 (Stevens, J. concurring). *See* Emily B. Rubin et al., *States Worse than Death among Hospitalized with Serious Illness*. Online August 1, 2016, at doi:10.1001/;amainternmed.2016.4362.

80. *See* George P. Smith, II, *Gently Into the Good Night: Toward a Compassionate Response to End-Stage Illness*, 22 TEMP. POLITICAL & CIVIL RIGHTS L. REV. 475, 488–89 (2013) (asserting that the Common Law right to refuse treatment is a more realistic option for attaining dignity at death than seeking to establish a constitutional right to die with dignity and with assistance).

81. 505 U.S. 833 (1992).

82. *Id.* at 851.

83. *Cruzan v. Mo. Dep't of Health*, 497 U.S. 261 (1990).

84. *Planned Parenthood v. Casey*, *supra* note 81.

85. *See* NEIL M. GORSUCH, THE FUTURE OF ASSISTED SUICIDE AND EUTHANASIA 18, 84, & Ch. 4 (2006).

86. It was determined in *Gonzales v. Oregon*, 546 U.S. 243 (2006) that states were allowed to make their own decisions regarding assisted suicide and, thus, that the Attorney General of the United States could not enforce the federal controlled substances law against physicians who prescribed drugs in compliance with the laws of the state of Oregon laws to terminally ill patients to end their lives.

87. *See* JOHN RAWLS, A THEORY OF JUSTICE (1971).

88. *See* JOHN STUART MILL, ON LIBERTY, Chs. III, IV (1859).

89. *See*, *The Right to Die*, THE ECONOMIST, Jan. 27, 2015, at 9.

90. *See* George P. Smith, II, *All's Well that Ends Well: Toward a Policy of Assisted Rational Suicide or Merely Enlightened Self-Determination?* 22 U. CAL. DAVIS L. REV. 275 (1989). *See also* HAZEL BIGGS, EUTHANASIA, DEATH WITH DIGNITY AND THE LAW (2001).

91. *See* RICHARD A. POSNER, AGING AND OLD AGE (1995). *See generally* VICTOR BROMBERT, MUSINGS ON MORTALITY (2013).

92. *See* RICHARD EPSTEIN, MORTAL PERIL; OUR INALIENABLE RIGHT TO HEALTH CARE? (1997).

93. *Obergefell v. Hodges*, 135 S. Ct. 2584, 2597 (2015).

94. *Id.* at 2597.

95. *Id.* at 2621.

96. *Id.* at 2596. *See generally* Mark Strasser, *Obergefell, Dignity and the Family*, 19 J GENDER, RACE & JUSTICE 317 (2016).

97. *Obergefell v. Hodges, id.* at 2596. It has been asserted that the notion of maintaining respect for human dignity as set forth in *Obergefell* surely implies equal respect, as well, for "diverse life styles." Peggy Cooper Davis, *Little Citizens and Their Families*, 43 FORDHAM URB. L. J. 1009, 1021 (2016).

98. *See generally Obergefell v. Hodges, id.* (discussing Justice Kennedy's position on the dignity of personhood); William N. Eskridge, Jr., *The Marriage Equality Cases and Constitutional Theory*, CATO SUP. CT. REV. 111 (2015) (analyzing the role of precedent in *Obergefell* and Chief Justice Roberts's concern, in his dissent, of Justice Kennedy's "recharacterization" of prior decisions by the Court).

99. ORE. REV. STAT. §§ 127.800 (12), 127.805 (2005); WASH. REV. CODE ANN. 70 245 (West 2009); 18 VT. STAT. ANN. Ch. 113, § 5281 (2013); CAL. HEALTH & SAFETY § 443.1 et. Seq. (2015); CO. REV. STAT. § 25-48-101 (2016); D.C. CODE §§ 7-661.01–7-661.17 (2017). *Presently*, some 25 states are considering similar legislative proposals. Josh Sanburn, *How Canada's Right-To-Die Ruling Could Boost Movement* in TIME, Feb. 6, 2015, at http://time.com/3699464,Feb62015. *See* Thaddeus M. Pope, *Legal History of Medical Aid in Dying: Physician Assisted Death in U.S. Courts and Legislatures*, 48 N. MEX. L. REV. 267 (2018). *See also* L. W. SUMNER, *supra* note 69, at Chs. 7, 10. *But see The Sorrows of Werther*, THE ECONOMIST, June 16, 2018, at 24 (suggesting ways to prevent suicide and to deal with melancholia). *See generally* Smith, *supra* note 90.

100. *Baxter v. Montana*, 354 MONT. 234 (2009). On January 13, 2014, Judge Nan G. Nash, of the Second Judicial Court, Bernalillo County, New Mexico, ruled terminally ill, mentally competent individuals have a constitutional right to request prescribed medication to shorten their suffering. *See Morris v. Brandenberg*. The Supreme Court of New Mexico reversed and found that there was no absolute and fundamental constitutional right to a physician's aid in dying and, consequently, accepted medical practices allowing aid in dying in cases of this nature were not allowed, *Morris v. Brandenberg*, __ N. M. __, 376 P. 3d 836 (2016).

101. *See* JOHN GRIFFITHS, HELEN WEYERS & MAURICE ADAMS, EUTHANASIA AND LAW IN EUROPE (2008); SELF-DETERMINATION, DIGNITY AND END-OF-LIFE CARE: REGULATING ADVANCE DIRECTIVES IN INTERNATIONAL AND COMPARATIVE PERSPECTIVES (Stefania Negri ed.,

2011). *See also* Scott Y. Kim, Raymond G. DeVries & John H. Peteet, *Euthanasia and Assisted Suicide of Patients with Psychiatric Disorders in the Netherlands*, J.A.M.A. Psychiatry, Feb. 10, 2016 at E1 *passim*, online (challenging the notion that an informed judgment can ever be given by an emotionally or cognitively impaired person). For a survey of attitudes regarding physician assistance from fifteen countries, *see Attitudes Towards Assisted Dying,* THE ECONOMIST, June 27, 2015 at 19. A new study has found that although euthanasia and physician suicide are becoming more accepted legally, their active use is rare and not subject to excessive abuse—confined primarily, as such, to patients with cancer. Ezekiel J. Emanuel et al., *Attitudes and Practices of Euthanasia, Physician-Assisted Suicide in the United States, Canada, and Europe*, 36 JAMA 79 (July 5, 2016). In *Carter v. Canada (Attorney General)*, 2015 SCC5, the Supreme Court of Canada reached a unanimous decision on February 6, 2015, which reversed a previous holding prohibiting laws allowing for physician assistance for patients in a terminal medical condition (*Rodriguez v. Br. Columbia (Attorney General)*) 1993. In *Carter*, the High Court held that any such prohibitions of this nature and the very notion that "grievous and irremediable medical conditions" can exist, which, for humane and compassionate medical reasons are not subject to relief, not only infringe on the right to life, liberty, and dignity and security, but are in contravention to fundamental principles of justice. Ian Austen, *Canada Court Strikes Down Ban on Aiding Patient Suicide*, N.Y. TIMES, Feb. 6, 2015, at 4. On June 18, 2016, the Parliament enacted legislation (Bill C-14) providing a right to assistance at death for citizens, 18 years or older, who suffer with a "grievous and irremediable" medical, including psychological, conditions. *See* Criminal Code, R.S.C. 1985, c.C-46, s 241.2(1)(c). The British, although having no parliamentary guidance by a specific law regulating assistance in dying (http://services.parliament.uk/bills12016-17/assisteddying.html), continue meddling, judicially, through this contentious medicolegal issue. *See* Smith, *supra* note 73 at 480-81, at nn. 62–66. *See generally Final Certainty,* THE ECONOMIST, June 27, 2015 at 16; *Loved to Death*, THE ECONOMIST, June 9, 2018 at 36 (discussing the challenges which China faces in only providing end-of-life care to less than 1 percent of its population).

102. Laurence H. Tribe, *Revising the Rule of Law*, 64 N.Y.U. L. REV. 726, 729 (1989).

103. *Id.*

104. *Id.*

105. Lynne N. Henderson, *Legality and Empathy*, 85 MICH. L. REV. 1574, 1579-82 (1987).

106. *See generally* JOHN NOONAN, PERSONS AND MASKS OF LAW (1976).

107. Benjamin Zipursky, DeShaney, and *The Jurisprudence of Compassion*, 65 N.Y.U. L. REV. 1101, 112 (1990).

108. Henderson, *supra* note 105 at 1588.

109. Smith, *supra* note 73 at 529. *See* STEPHEN W. SMITH, END-OF-LIFE DECISIONS IN MEDICAL CARE: PRINCIPLES AND POLICES FOR REGULATING THE DYING PROCESS (2012).

110. *Id.*

111. RICHARD A. POSNER, HOW JUDGES THINK, at 117 (2008) (emphasis added).

112. Laurence H. Tribe, *Lawrence v. Texas: The Fundamental Right That Dare Not Speak Its Name*, 117 HARV. L. REV. 1893, 1935–36 (2004).

113. *Id.* at 1936.

114. *Id.*

115. *Planned Parenthood of Southeastern Pa. v. Casey*, 505 U.S. 833, 851 (1992).

116. *See Lawrence v. Texas*, 539 U.S. 558, 573, 578 (2003). Even though a patient's autonomous needs are central to a therapeutic dialogue, there are a growing number of cases where—for reasons of conscience—a physician, because of religious or moral reasons, objects to following a course of action (e.g., abortion, assistance at death) requested by a patient. Personal objections are being allowed in health care service more and more by state legislative design. *See* Wesley J. Smith, *"Obliged to Kill" The Assault on Medical Conscience*, THE WEEKLY STANDARD, Mar. 12, 2018, at 21. *Best see* Ronit Y. Stahl & Ezekiel J. Emanuel, *Physicians, Not Conscripts—Conscientious Objection is Health Care*, 376 NEW ENG. J. MED. 1380 (April 6, 2017).

117. *Casey*, 505 U.S. at 850. The right of privacy from governmental intrusions, expressed in *Griswold and Eisenstadt*, add to the strength of the liberty of associational expression found in Lawrence, in arguing for a right to die with dignity without unduly burdensome state interference. *See Eisenstadt v. Baird*, 405 U.S. 438 (1972); *Griswold v. Connecticut*, 381 U.S. 479 (1965).

118. DAVID C. THOMASMA, HUMAN LIFE IN THE BALANCE at 195 (1990).

119. *Id.* This duty should be triggered when one is diagnosed as terminally ill, has made a determination (or executed an advance directive) that, because of medical conditions, life no longer has personal meaning or, when, even though no such decision has been made by the patient and there is no advance directive, there is nonetheless a medical realization that the terminal illness is "in its imminent phase." *Id.* at 194.

120. EDMUND D. PELLEGRINO & DAVID C. THOMASMA, FOR THE PATIENT'S OWN GOOD: THE RESTORATION OF BENEFICENCE IN HEALTH CARE (1988).

121. Eric J. Cassell, *The Nature of Suffering and The Glory of Medicine*, 306 NEW ENG. J. MED. 639 (1982).

122. Smith, *supra* note 73 at 530–31.

123. *Id.*

124. *Id.* at 487. *See* STEPHEN W. SMITH, *supra* note 109.

125. Smith, *supra* note 73 at 488.

126. GEORGE P. SMITH, II, Monograph, WHEN MERCY SEASONS JUSTICE at 21 (2007).

127. Minette Marrin, *Opinion, An Acceptable Way to Arrange Our Death*, THE SUNDAY TIMES, May 14, 2006, at 18.

128. *Id.*

129. *Id. See* BARBARA EHRENREICH, NATURAL CAUSES (2018) (arguing against wider uses of medical, physical, and "unnatural" interventions designed to prolong life and well-being at any cost and, instead, encouraging acceptance of life's finitude and thus stressing its full enjoyment, no matter its duration).

Chapter 4

Dignity in Domestic and in International Context: Aspirations, Limited Successes, and the Legacy of Senator Bricker

As seen in the United States and some other countries, human dignity "remains in the background as a value justifying the set of human rights, but does not operate as an applicable legal rule at all."[1] While a natural law theory of rights was asserted in the Declaration of Independence, it was not repeated—expressly—in the Preamble or found within operative provisions of the Constitution itself.[2] Specifically, since the conclusion of World War II, judicial reasoning has embraced the principle of human dignity as a means of interpreting enumerated rights "without producing any positive right or enforceable principle of human dignity."[3]

Pursuing efforts to understand the doctrinal concept of human dignity can be enhanced if a link is recognized between the concept and its pertinence with the Bill of Rights. Such a recognition will have the effect, it is argued, of re-enforcing "the liberty expressly and practically enshrined in the Bill of Rights."[4] From both majority and minority case opinions in the U.S. Supreme Court, human dignity is seen clearly as a constitutional value considered when interpreting the "various rights enshrined in the Bill of Rights."[5] Indeed, judicial history shows that dignity is not only an underlying value in First Amendment cases, but the Fourth through the Eighth Amendments.[6]

DOMESTIC APPLICATIONS IN THE UNITED STATES

Dignity has become a part of the vocabulary of constitutional rights only within the last sixty to seventy years.[7] The word has been referenced not only to individuals, nations, and states, but with legal institutions, personage, the flag, and even God.[8] It was not until the 1940s, however, that the U.S.

Supreme Court acknowledged and then embraced dignity "as something possessed by individuals."[9]

As observed, since dignity, as a concept, is not fixed ideologically, it has no uniformly accepted meaning—this, because it is used differently from various perspectives.[10] The context—political, moral or legal, and legislative or judicial—in which dignity is applied determines the extent to which it becomes "operationalized."[11] Typically, whether dignity is a right, principle, norm, or value depends largely upon whether it is seen as a negative, or as a positive, obligation.[12] Thus, it may be concretized "as a negative right against other persons or the state," or—alternatively—as a positive obligation (particularly on the state.)"[13] If characterized as a negative obligation, then an evaluation of its narrowness must be made and a determination reached whether it is properly viewed as a "prohibition on humiliating others, or more."[14] If it is deemed a positive obligation, then the extent of its breadth must be assessed.[15] If dignity is taken as an absolute value or as a right, and thereby defined broadly, the more courts will be prevented from seeking to balance competing values.[16]

At its highest level as an ideal, dignity becomes a conduit for dialogue.[17] Dignity provides "a language in which conflicting values and rights can be brought into relationship with each other."[18] It can not only be used as a tool to combat discrimination, but as a means of "fleshing out" the level of constitutional protection needed in order to provide a "basic protection" from political and utilitarian calculations. This protection, in turn, allows dignity to be a construct for expanding the notion of empathy.[19]

The Principle of Anti-Humiliation: A New Strategy for Litigating

In America, equality and liberty are the two central concepts upon which constitutional traditions are anchored.[20] And, because of this status, constitutional lawyers have difficulty in seeing—and then establishing—a link between human dignity and the principle of anti-humiliation.[21] The United Supreme Court has, however, come close to validating this principle through its use of the very term, "dignity," in more than 900 opinions since 1789—with significant numbers being seen since the 1940s.[22] Interestingly, the phrase "human dignity," was first used by the Supreme Court by Justice Frank W. Murphy in a dissenting opinion in the case of *In re Yamashita* in 1946.[23] The scope of application for dignity cases runs from education equality,[24] prison conditions,[25] abortions,[26] and partial abortions,[27] to gay rights[28] and interracial marriage.[29] It is within contemporary LGBTQ issues where individuals of this character are among the most common victims of humiliation.[30] For the judiciary, the link with dignity and with anti-humiliation should be neither complicated nor onerous—but rather intuitive, since the opposite of humiliation is dignity.[31]

Prevailing social practices should play a significant part in judicial decision making.[32] Common, or "situation" sense judgments, should be a means of reaching a just result.[33] Of necessity, these judgments are formed and tested by use of Brandeis Briefs.[34] Justice Louis Brandeis authored a Supreme Court opinion in the case of *Mueller v. Oregon* in 1908,[35] which was recognized as the very first case in American Legal History to go outside legal citations made in the case briefs and then proceed to shape the ultimate decision based on scientific information and the social sciences.[36] These two approaches to informal decision making—use by the judiciary of a "situation sense" and deference to the Brandeis Brief—form the foundation for a new construct for constitutional analyses of civil rights protection.[37]

As observed, dignity's antonym is humiliation and includes "other aspects of social exclusion, lowering of social status, and denials of recognition."[38] Under a new construct for analysis, designated the Ackerman Anti-Humiliation Principle, "institutionalized humiliation" is seen to be the "distinctive wrong of racism" and traces its provenance to the opinion of the Supreme Court written by Chief Justice Earl Warren in *Brown v. Board of Education* in 1954.[39] Put directly, the Ackerman Principle gives rise to a process for discerning humiliation, which, itself, finds force from two sources: a judge's "situation-sense" and "Brandeis Briefs."[40]

Shaping a definition of what the components of institutionalized humiliation forces a first order definition of "personal humiliation."[41] Ackerman defines personal humiliation as a "face-to-face insult in which the victim acquiesces in the effort to impugn his standing as a minimally competent actor within a particular sphere of life."[42] The institutionalization of harm of this nature is, then, amplified in its effect. Face-to-face interaction may not always be necessary to prove harm of this degree because—for example—signage such as "No Negroes Allowed," or "norms expressing the same sentiment, could achieve the same result."[43]

To come within the protection of the anti-humiliation principle, it remains for a complaining party to show that he accepted, rather than denied, the affront.[44] Additionally, the individual's minimal competence within a particular sphere of life activity must be a part of the affront.[45] Finally, an actionable affront need not—although it may—apply "across the board."[46] Actual civil rights trials are seen as an excellent—although underutilized—method for establishing institutionalized humiliation.[47] Trials of this nature have one particular strength: they allow experts on institutionalized humiliation, such as psychologists, scientists, and historians, to "conceptualize" the individual voices of the moving party or parties.[48]

LIMITING THE SCOPE OF INTERNATIONAL INFLUENCES

Noble though the Charter of the United Nations is, it reveals points of tension between human rights and sovereignty.[49] Although the sovereign rights of autonomy held by the members of the U.N. are acknowledged and respected within their own jurisdictions, the Charter also places limits on "absolute sovereignty."[50] Specifically, Article 55 of the Charter declares that the manner in which states treat their inhabitants is of international concern—especially in the promotion and the protection of broad human rights principles: to advance higher standards of living; maintain international economic, social, health, education and cultural values; and show universal respect for human rights and fundamental freedoms.[51] Article 56 requires the member states to "pledge" themselves to support these principles, thereby—in effect—relinquishing a significant part of state autonomy over the populations within their individual boundaries.[52] Ceding large portions of state sovereignty to one world union is problematic for many in the United States, for example.[53] As observed, the Charter is recognized as the foundational text from which the Universal Declaration of Human Rights derives and the basis of authority for the Covenants on Civil and Political Rights and on Economic, Social, and Cultural Rights—this, even though it is not a part of the International Bill of Human Rights.[54]

Introducing concepts of equality and self-determination and then proceeding to set rules for delineating "appropriate social, political, and economic relationships between states and among populations" was a source of hope for those living in colonial dependencies.[55] It was also an issue of concern for colonial powers—for, the very notion of human rights "threatened the internal structuring of their colonial empires."[56] It was not until 1960 that a U.N. Resolution was passed which granted independence to colonial territories.[57] In 1966, the General Assembly of the U.N. adopted the Covenants.[58]

The history of so-called fundamental and universal rights shows clearly that these rights are not so much universal in their character or—for that matter, Western or Eastern in origin—but, that they have risen from "interdependent relationships of duties and rights,"[59] and from struggles over social ordering.[60] In subsequent years to the formation of the U.N., countless dedicated human rights treaties have been drafted.[61] Yet, at the time of the Charter's ratification, this instrument "was the only binding international agreement that mentioned human rights the United States has ratified."[62]

Judicial and Political Concerns: The Bricker Amendment

Beginning in 1948, with the case of *Oyoma v. California*,[63] and followed by *Hurd v. Hodge*,[64] provisions within the U.N. Charter were referenced in these two case decisions. While not treating the Charter as binding, these cases were seen as "an emerging trend toward accepting international principles in domestic life"—and quite possibly relinquishing local mores for those of the broader, global community.[65]

In 1952, with the case of *Fujii v. State of California*,[66] the Charter was used for the first (and most likely the only) time to *invalidate* a domestic law on the grounds of a human rights violation.[67] This decision became a catalyst for mobilizing concern that international human rights was becoming superior to domestic law.[68] Indeed, this decision "sent shockwaves through the legal and political communities" and galvanized opposition to the notion of internationalism.[69]

These judicial events set the tone for an effort launched by U.S. Senator John Bricker of Ohio in 1953 designed to amend the U.S. Constitution in order to restrict both the power and the execution of international human rights treaties.[70] Although these efforts failed, President Dwight D. Eisenhower decided not to make an attempt to ratify the two Covenants.[71] In 1992, the Senate ratified the International Covenant on Civil and Political Rights, but with five revisions and four Declarations.[72] Although signed by President Carter in 1979, the Covenant on Economic, Social, and Cultural Rights has yet to be ratified by the Senate.[73]

More than sixty years later, the spirit of the movement led by Senator Bricker continues as an effort to define both the nature and the limits of the United States approach to human rights.[74] Today, in America, human rights are often presumed to be "an international phenomenon, void of much domestic influence or provenance."[75] Indeed, these rights are seen as little more than "export commodities—goods shipped off to others in far away places, but rarely considered fit for domestic consumption."[76] Stated otherwise, presently there simply is no normative legitimacy of human rights to be found within a "domestic United States context."[77]

A Perplexing Legacy

Still today, the extent to which the U.S. Supreme Court utilizes international law norms in substantive constitutional interpretations is a volatile issue of debate.[78] While considered proper for the use of such norms for expository or empirical purposes, the fact that foreign or international bodies have adopted a particular rule as reason to constitutionalize and thereby afford substantive meaning to the U.S. Constitution is thought to be without justification.[79] This type of moral fact finding has been soundly denounced by the late Justice Antonin Scalia as improper—simply because American law has different moral and legal frameworks than those found within international law.[80] Surely, however, there are universally shared common values such as human dignity, compassion, and humaneness, which are important core values or even "norms" of conduct in some cases that form a part of the civilized conscience of mankind and which should never be excluded from being vectors of force in judicial decision making much as in the same way equity is ever present in all systems of law—domestic and international.[81]

NOTES

1. Gerald L. Neuman, Ch. 39, *Discourses of Dignity*, at 640 in UNDERSTANDING HUMAN DIGNITY (Christopher McCrudden ed., 2013) [hereinafter UNDERSTANDING DIGNITY].

2. *Id.*

3. *Id.* at 641. *See* Alan Gewirth, *Human Dignity, as a Basis of Rights* in THE CONSTITUTION OF RIGHTS: HUMAN DIGNITY AND AMERICAN VALUES at 10, 11–14 (Michael J. Meyer & William A. Parent eds., 1992) (where a distinction is drawn between conceptions of dignity which recognize the capacity of persons to make claims against others and the alternative position that places dignity as an inherent, priceless antecedent to rights). *See also*, Dieter Grimm, Ch. 21, *Dignity in a Legal Context: Dignity as an Absolute Right*, at 38 in UNDERSTANDING DIGNITY, *supra* note 1.

4. AHARON BARAK, HUMAN DIGNITY: THE CONSTITUTIONAL VALUE AND THE CONSTITUTIONAL RIGHT 206–08 (2015).

5. *Id.* at 198.

6. *Id.* at 198–99. *See* Maxine D. Goodman, *Human Dignity in the Supreme Court Jurisprudence*, 84 NEB. L. REV. 740, 743 (2006).

7. Judith Resnik & Julie C. Suk, *Adding Insult to Injury: Questioning the Role of Dignity in Conceptions of Sovereignty*, 55 STAN. L. REV. 1921 (2003).

8. *Id.* at 1934–36.

9. *Id.* at 1934. In 1942, and the case of *Glasser v. United States*, 315 U.S. 60, 89, Justice Felix Frankfurter—in dissent—acknowledged that a central tenet of a democratic society is "respect for the dignity of all men." While contemporary rulings by the U.S. Supreme Court have invoked dignity as a concept for protecting or even recognizing, fundamental rights for the marginalized, advocates of racial justice should be cautious in advocating dignity as a viable construct for decision-making. The Equal Protection Doctrine is seen as a stronger force for the protection of privileged classes than to disadvantaged groups—this, especially since the Court has yet to recognize the stigmatizing nature of *defacto* discrimination. Darren L. Hutchinson, *Undignified: The Supreme Court, Racial Justice, and Dignity Claims*, 69 FLA. L. REV. 1, 2–43 (2017).

10. Christopher McCrudden, Ch. 1, *In Pursuit of Human Dignity*, at 10 in UNDERSTANDING DIGNITY, *supra* note 1.

11. Christopher Mollers, Ch. 9, *The Triple Dilemma of Human Dignity: A Case Study*, at 173 in UNDERSTANDING DIGNITY, *supra* note 1.

12. McCrudden, *supra* note 10 at 50.

13. *Id.*
14. *Id.*
15. *Id.*
16. *Id.* at 51. *See* SANDRA FREDMAN, HUMAN RIGHTS TRANSFORMED: POSITIVE RIGHTS AND POSITIVE DUTIES (2008).
17. McCRUDDEN, *supra* note 10 at 13.
18. *Id.* at 14. *See generally* Hutchinson, *supra* note 9.
19. McCRUDDEN, *supra* note 10 at 13.
20. Kenji Yoshino, *The Anti-Humiliation Principle and Same Sex Marriage*, 123 YALE, L. J. 3077, 3082 (2014).
21. *Id.* at 3087.
22. *See* Leslie M. Henry, *The Jurisprudence of Dignity*, 160 U. PA. L. REV. 160, 178–79 (2011). *See also* Resnick & Sulk, *supra* note 7 at 1933; Jordan J. Paust, *Human Dignity as a Constitutional Right: A Jurisprudentially Based Inquiry into Criteria and Content*, 27 HOWARD L. J. 145, 150 *passim* (1989).
23. In re *Yamashita*, 327 U.S. 1, 29 (1946) (Murphy, J. dissenting).
24. *Brown v. Bd. of Education*, 347 U.S. 483 (1954).
25. *Brown v. Plata*, 131 S. Ct. 1910, 1928 (2011).
26. *Planned Parenthood of Se. Pa. v. Casey*, 505 U.S. 833 (1991).
27. *Gonzales v. Carhart*, 550 U.S. 124, 157 (2007).
28. *U.S. v. Windsor*, 133 S. Ct. 2675 (2013); *Lawrence v. Texas*, 539 U.S. 558 (2003).
29. *Loving v. Virginia*, 388 U.S. 1 (1967).
30. Yoshino, *supra* note 20.
31. *Id. But see* Noah Lindell, 27 CORNELL J. L. & PUB. POL'Y 27 (2017) (arguing that since dignity is a constitutional value, rather than a right, and thus has no place in statutory interpretation, the courts should create a dignity canon of interpretation which would be operable as a clear statement rule; accordingly, it would be for the legislatures to expressly designate when actions may be undertaken which limit individual dignity).
32. *See* KARL LLEWELLYN, THE COMMON LAW TRADITION: DECIDING APPEALS at 122 (1960).
33. *Id. See* BENJAMIN N. CARDOZO, THE NATURE OF THE JUDICIAL PROCESS 218 (1921) (where reference to prevailing social usages and customs are listed as one of four methods which "should" be utilized by courts in judicial decision making). *See also* RICHARD A. POSNER, HOW JUDGES THINK, Ch. 1 (2008).
34. Yoshino, supra note 20 at 3088–091. *See* Patrick J. Rohan, *The Common Law Tradition: "Just Result" Jurisprudence?* 32 FORDHAM L. REV. 51, 56 (1963).
35. 208 U.S. 412 (1908).
36. Yoshino, *supra* note 20 at 3088–091; Rohan, *supra* note 34.
37. Yoshino, *supra* note 20 at 3088 *passim*. *See* 3 BRUCE ACKERMAN, WE THE PEOPLE: THE CIVIL RIGHTS REVOLUTION at 128 (2014).
38. Doron Shultziner & Itai Rabinovici, *Human Dignity, Self-Worth and Humiliation: A Comparative Legal-Psychological Approach*, 18 PSYCHOLOGY, PUB. POL'Y & L. 105–06 (2012).

39. *Brown v. Bd. of Education*, *supra* note 24.
40. Yoshino, *supra* note 20 at 3088.
41. *Id.*
42. ACKERMAN, *supra* note 37 at 138.
43. *Id. See* Lindell, *supra* note 31.
44. *Id.*
45. ACKERMAN, *supra* note 37 at 140.
46. Yoshino, *supra* note 20 at 3092–93.
47. *Id.*
48. *Id.*
49. CHRISTOPHER N. J. ROBERTS, THE CONTENTIOUS HISTORY OF THE INTERNATIONAL BILL OF RIGHTS 77 (2014). *See* Appendix A, *infra.*
50. ROBERTS, *id.*
51. *Id.*
52. *Id.*
53. *Id.* at 81.
54. *Id.* at 78.
55. *Id.* at 123.
56. *Id. See* Appendices A, B, C, D, *infra.*
57. ROBERTS, *supra* note 49 at 227.
58. *Id.*
59. *Id.* at 151.
60. *Id.* at 227.
61. *Id.* at 88.
62. *Id.* at 88.
63. 332 U.S. 633 (1948) (per Black & per Douglas, J's).
64. 334 U.S. 24 (1948) (per Vinson, C. J.)
65. ROBERTS, *supra* note 49 at 101.
66. 242 P.2d 617 (Cal. 1952).
67. ROBERTS, *supra* note 49 at 113.
68. *Id.* at 115 *passim.*
69. *Id.* at 117.
70. *Id.* at 73, 225–26. The Bricker Amendment to the Constitution consisted of four succinct sections. "Section 1: A provision of a treaty which conflicts with this constitution shall not be of any force or effect; Section 2: No treaty shall authorize or permit any foreign power or any international organization to supervise, control, or adjudicate rights of citizens of the United States within the United States enumerated in this constitution or any other matter essentially within the domestic jurisdiction of the United States; Section 3: A treaty shall become effective as internal law in the United States only through the enactment of appropriation legislation by the Congress; Section 4: All executive and other agreements between the President and any international organization, foreign power, or official thereof shall be made only in the manner and to the extent to be prescribed by law. Such agreements shall be subject to the limitations imposed on treaties, or the making of treaties, by this Article." (S. J. Res. 130, Feb. 7, 1950).

71. ROBERTS, *supra* note 49, at 226.

72. *See* Kristina Ash, *U.S. Reservations to the International Covenant on Civil and Political Rights: Credibility and Maximization and Global Influence* 3 N. W. J. INT'L HUMAN RTS. 1 (2005).

73. *See* Ann Piccard, *The United States' Failure to Ratify the International Covenant on Economic, Social and Cultural Rights: Must the Poor Be Always with Us?* 13 ST. MARY'S L. REV. MINORITY RTS. 231 (2010).

74. ROBERTS, *supra* 49, at 73.

75. *Id.* at 120.

76. *Id.* at 121.

77. Christopher N. J. Roberts, *Human Rights Law: The (Re)making of an American Story*, 26 MINN. J. INT'L L. 1, 51 (2017).

78. *See* STEPHEN BREYER, THE COURT AND THE WORLD: AMERICAN LAW AND THE NEW GLOBAL REALITIES (2015) (asserting U.S. laws should be harmonized with foreign treaties and laws). *But see*, Note, *Constitutional Courts and International Law: Revisiting the Transatlantic Divide*, 129 HARV. L. REV. 1362 (2016) (analyzing the supremacy of constitutional law over international law in Europe and America and the procedural difficulties incorporating international law into domestic law in America—concluding, as such, both transatlantic partners have developed mechanisms to prevent domestic law from being compromised by international law, yet acknowledging a recent European Court of Justice decision which designates certain fundamental rights as "extraordinary" constitutional principles which—unlike "normal" constitutional provisions—supersede incompatible international norms). *See generally* Joan L. Larsen, *Importing Control Norms from a "Wider Civilization": Lawrence and the Rehnquist Court's Use of Foreign and International Law in Domestic Constitutional Interpretation*, 65 OHIO ST. L. J. 1283 (2004) (discussing the extent to which SCOTUS uses international law norms in substantive constitutional interpretations).

79. *See* Larsen, *supra* note 78, at 1287; *see also Lawrence v. Texas*, 539 U.S. 558, 576 (2003) (referencing the holdings of the European Court of Human Rights). *See also* Roper v. Simmons, 543 U.S. 551 (2005).

80. Roper, 543 U.S. at 608, 622 *passim* (Scalia, J. dissenting); *see* Roger P. Alford, *Misusing International Sources to Interpret the Constitution*, 98 AM. J. INT'L L. 57 (2004). *But see* Ian M. Kysel, *Domesticating Human Rights Norms in the United States: Considering the Role and Obligations of the Federal Government as Litigant*, 46 GEO. J. INT'L L. 1009 (2015); Ralph G. Steinhardt, *Determining Which Human Rights Claims "Touch and Concern" the United States: Justice Kennedy's Filartiga*, 89 NOTRE DAME L. REV. 1695 (2014); Penny M. Venetis, *Enforcing Human Rights in the United States: Which Tribunals are Best Suited to Adjudicate Treaty-Based Claims?* 23 S. CAL. REV. L. & SOC. JUST. 121 (2014).

81. *See* MARK W. JANIS, AN INTRODUCTION TO INTERNATIONAL LAW 53–66 (3rd ed., 1999).

Chapter 5

Implementing or Impeding Dignity: Subsidiarity and Proportionality

Subsidiarity

As a structural principle of international human rights law and as an ideal, subsidiarity is—quite directly—a model of social organization.[1] It became a part of the political lexicon in the twentieth century, but traces its provenance to classical Greece.[2] Implied within this principle is a notion that there be a "requisite degree of normative coherence in the larger community" in order to facilitate the "functions of assisting, protecting, coordinating and unifying."[3] Stated otherwise, subsidiarity is formulated as a principle of justice that requires large communities to recognize and protect the legitimacy of autonomy within small communities and to render a level of assistance to them when needed—this, in order to advance and preserve the common good of the larger community.[4] Indeed, the object of all justice is to stabilize and safeguard the common good.[5]

The efficiency of subsidiarity is not found from it as being a force for social efficiency or even as a template for political compromise. Rather, its etiology is "personalistic rather than contractual or utilitarian."[6] At bottom, subsidiarity, then, is to be acknowledged as "a conviction that each human individual is endowed with an inherent and inalienable worth, or dignity, and thus the value of the individual human person is ontologically and morally prior to the state or other social groupings.[7]

Both subsidiarity and human rights seek to advance and to secure the common dignity of the human person.[8] Noble though the principle of subsidiarity is, procedures for safeguarding its implementation through human rights guarantees and protections remain illusionary—this, because the law of human rights, itself, is subject to long-standing incoherence and inconsistency.[9] The inability of subsidiarity may be understood further when law is accepted as being more than a "system of rules" set within one "normative universe" rather than seen correctly as being comprised of plural communities that have countless "narratives that locate law and give it meaning" within those communities.[10]

The requirement of normative coherence for the principle of subsidiarity to be operative is, sadly, not found today within international law.[11] Taken as a whole, this absence or even a minimal semblance of coherence, results in subsidiarity being severely compromised as an operative principle.[12] Today, international law is "essentially a multiplicity of functionally sectoral regulatory arrangements,"[13] and is viewed as "highly fragmented" and "uncoordinated."[14]

Norms—and here dignity—develop from behaviorism,[15] which, in turn focuses on those social conditions[16] that either enable or disable various life actions. Normative environments must, of necessity, be seen as being composed of economic, social, cultural, civil, and political actions or vectors of force.[17] Strong arguments have been made that, because of their ethical universality, certain norms governing human rights (such as dignity) should be recognized as enjoying a superior status, which, in turn, means that they should have a priority in sectoral regulations and not be classified as subordinate to other norms.[18]

Unless and until international law develops stronger evaluative criteria for determining when states should be accorded autonomy and when sovereignty should give way to subsidiary-based intervention, international legal theory will continue to chart a stark decline of state consent—with the consequence being that the "nonconsensual norms based on global community values" will prevail.[19]

International human rights treaties that endeavor to structure regulatory regimes are generally ineffective because they ignore the realities of individual state behaviorism and seek to have human rights enforced by treaty and/or universal declarations.[20] Since there is no central enforcement mechanism for violations of human rights, the whole corpus of international human rights law must be acknowledged as "hopelessly weak" because of this failure.[21] Ultimately, whether state actions comply with a particular treaty or allow a state to first recognize, and then endeavor to realize, provisions of universal declarations, depend upon the social conditions within each state.[22]

It is encouraging to observe that over the last decade, the justiciability of economic, social, and cultural rights has been evolving.[23] The effect of this recognition for human rights is that they are now open to interpretation by judicial or quasi-judicial bodies and, furthermore, determinations may be made regarding the sufficiency of a complaint before these bodies for violations of these rights.[24]

Generally, the right to human dignity, when recognized judicially, is not absolute.[25] Rather, it is classified as relative and may thus, be limited.[26] The limitations placed on constitutional rights are held applicable, equally, to the right to human dignity.[27] Accordingly, the law of proportionately does not recognize every limitation or restriction of the human dignity right as unconstitutional.[28] "Only a disproportionate limitation of human dignity is unconstitutional."[29] In Germany, however, the law of proportionately is inapplicable to human dignity which is seen as absolute.[30] No constitutional amendment to this German right is, thus, allowed.[31] Adopted in 1949, The Basic Law of Germany begins with the words, "Human dignity shall be inviolable. To respect and protect it shall be the duty of all state authority."[32] Today, Germans agree—commonly—that The Basic Law is fundamentally "a normative constitution embracing values."[33] Previously, the understanding was that the Constitution was but a "simple expression of an existential order of power."[34]

In 1992, Israel enacted the Basic Law: Human Dignity and Liberty, and thereby conferred constitutional status to both the value and to the right to human dignity. Subsequently, dignity was no longer to be viewed as but an "underlying declaratory principle or value."[35] Indeed, "the interpretation of 'dignity' thus became a necessity, carrying substantial legal consequences."[36]

A number of constitutions treat human dignity as both negative and positive.[37] Consequently, under the negative aspect, state obligations are not taken to be satisfied merely because restraints are in place that prevent the very imposition of limitations on the right to human dignity.[38] Consistent with the positive character of the right, the state must take "action to protect human dignity and facilitate its realization."[39]

JUDICIAL FORUMS

Two judicial bodies—the European Court of Human Rights[40] and the Inter-American Court of Human Rights[41]—are charged, respectively, with monitoring and protecting the human rights of 800 million Europeans and, with the support of the International Commission on Human Rights, maintaining a system of protection for the Organization of American States, which, itself, was founded on the principle of safeguarding the fundamental rights of the individual.[42] Yet, interestingly, there is no single international adjudicative body charged specifically with enforcing international humanitarian law for the regulation of armed conflict.[43] Rather, a fragmented variety of judicial bodies deal with violations of this nature.[44] The present situation exists, in large measure, because international humanitarian law is recognized as a body of law enforceable by the states.[45] Another fundamental weakness of humanitarian law is that it lacks any binding enforcement provisions.[46] Judicial complexities often arise when human rights tribunals—such as the Inter-American Commission and the Court of Human Rights—are presented with options to enforce international humanitarian law and to enforce human rights laws as well.[47]

A thoughtful and significant review of the contributions made by the European Court and the Inter-American Court shows judicial movement toward the increased humanization of international law.[48] Without doubt, a major doctrinal contribution has been made by Judge Antonio A. Cancado Trindade of Brazil toward the achievement of this goal of judicial decision-making. First, as a member of the Inter-American Court of Human Rights and presently a member of the International Court of Justice, Judge Trindade has sought to present a "dynamic . . . evolutive interpretative of the respective human rights conventions."[49] Elevating this body of norms though *jus cogens*—focused traditionally on purely inter-State relations—to a more responsive level where individuals and their suffering (projected in time) become a primary concern,[50] is laudable and, indeed, visionary.[51]

A review of some 600 judgments by the European Court of Human Rights has revealed that the word "dignity" has been used primarily in circumstances where—within the context of Article 3 of the European Convention on Human Rights—issues of physical or mental harm had been inflicted.[52] Article 3 prohibits torture together with "inhumane or degrading treatment or punishment."[53] What this survey shows clearly is that the concept of dignity, as presented to the European Court and accepted by the forty-seven countries who are parties to the European Convention on Human Rights, is that agreement as to violations of dignity are "related to experiences of physical or psychological suffering.[54] The case law before the European Court of Human Rights, then, shows indisputably that violations of dignity occur "when an individual is subjected to various kinds of physical or psychological abuse, the latter referring to subjective feelings . . . of humiliation and debasement, which are in effect various aspects of injuries to self-worth."[55] Indeed, at the very heart of self-worth is a need to afford protection from being insulted and humiliated.[56]

PROPORTIONALITY AND JUDICIAL REVIEW

Rather than present and advocate strong liberal views of rights, the modern constitutions chose to emphasize values[57] and community needs over the individual.[58] While rights are anchored with a value system, there are major differences between constitutional values and constitutional rights.[59] At its most basic level, "a value is a concept or standard considered worthwhile or desirable.[60] It reflects a level of responsiveness to both social and political causes but does hold specific content.[61] Contrariwise, a right usually defines relationships between the individual and the state—by use of entitlements—to be either "free from interference (in a negative sense) or to demand practical goods or services in the positive sense.[62] The post–World War II constitutions sought to "establish a balance between rights and between fundamental values"[63]; but with a decided emphasis being placed on values rather than a liberal view of rights as was done in the United States Constitution.[64] Rights under these new constitutions were to be limited, if not constrained, by values.[65]

The new constitutions centered human dignity as a core value, if not the very "foundation for the protection of rights" (especially human rights).[66] At the time of their enactments, these constitutions embodied both the preferences and the ideological commitments of modern European politics.[67]

In the United States, rights are seen as a bulwark of strength and protection against majoritarian policies. When the United States Supreme Court finds political necessities outweigh rights, these actions are seen as but exceptions to the overall scheme of a rights-based society.[68] The philosophy of the new constitutions, however, conceived of rights "as part of a general compromise with other political interests."[69]

"Proportionality review turns not so much on right but on the interests that might outweigh them."[70] As a consequence of this philosophy, the ability of courts to allow interests to "trump" rights is made easier.[71] Many of the limitations clauses in modern constitutions require—as a part of means-end analysis—that a balanced or proportional review be undertaken judicially when constitutional challenges arise.[72] These clauses direct the courts to "balance or weigh individual rights against governmental or social interests."[73] The generic idea of proportionality holds that there must be some minimal "fit" between actions and consequences or between ends and means in law.[74] Because of this dynamic, some have presupposed that proportionality analysis and balancing are a fundamental norm of *Grundnorm* in contemporary rights adjudication.[75]

The United States Position

The Preamble to the United States Constitution states explicitly that one of its goals is to "establish Justice."[76] Since the time of Aristotle, justice has been associated with proportionality.[77] Other antecedents to the Constitution—both in Magna Carta and the English Bill of Rights, for example—stress the needs of government to be just and exercise proportionality in the treatment of its citizens.[78]

In a constitutional democracy, proportionality should enjoy a special status relationship within the democracy. This situation arises when it is realized that the "essential idea of Constitutional democracy is that in confrontations between citizens and government, [the] government is restrained and avoids oppressive and arbitrary actions."[79] While the means of achieving this goal are varied, "requiring proportionality of action is one way the idea of limited government can be recognized."[80] Even though the principle of proportionality is part of the U.S. Constitution,[81] presently, structured proportionality is not used in American courts.[82] A clear textual basis for adopting proportionality as a pervasive test, is not provided in the Constitution as it is in Canada, for example.[83] This doctrine, as seen, developed in the post–World War II period in Germany, Canada, Israel, the United Kingdom, and other nation-states.[84]

Proportionality cannot be applied routinely to all constitutional rights.[85] Some rights can simply be better understood "as concrete rules, requiring particular procedures to legalize" the use of coercive power by the government.[86] Other rights are viewed more practically as "normally non-derogable guarantees,"[87] such as individualized rights against torture.[88] There is no uniform conceptual structure for all rights.[89] Similarly, not "all rights play the same role within the constitutional system."[90] Some rights such as those tested under the Establishment Clause, the 5th Amendment Takings Clause and the "blindness to differences among crimes" under the 4th Amendment and in criminal sentencing, could profit if a structured proportionality analysis were to be used.[91] Determining whether an area directs the need to be more categorical or is best served by a case-by-case application of standards of proportionality, is a major judicial task.[92]

NOTES

1. Paolo G. Carrozza, *Subsidiarity as a Structural Principle of International Human Rights Law*, 97 AM. J. INT'L L. 38 (2003).

2. *Id.*

3. Paolo G. Carrozza, *The Problematic Applicability of Subsidiarity to International Law*, 61 AM. J. JURIS. 51 *passim*, 56 (2016).

4. *Id.* at 54.

5. John Finnis, *Subsidiarity's Roots and History: Some Observations*, 61 AM. J. JURIS. 133 *passim* (2016). *See* Paolo G. Carrozza, *The Universal Common Good and The Authority of International Law*, 9 LOGOS 28 (2006).

6. Carrozza, *supra* note 1 at 40–41. The dignity of human beings constitutes the central reason for the very existence and justification for political organization. Rex D. Glensy, *The Right to Dignity*, 43 COLUM. HUM. RTS. L. Rev. 65, 72 (2011).

7. *Id.*

8. Carrozza, *supra* note 1 at 42. *See generally* GLOBAL PERSPECTIVES ON SUBSIDIARITY (Michelle Evans & Augusto Zimmerman eds., 2014).

9. Carrozza, *supra* note 1 at 42. *See* DINAH SHELTON, REMEDIES IN INTERNATIONAL HUMAN RIGHTS LAW at 1 (2nd ed., 2005). *See generally*

LITIGATING HEALTH RIGHTS: CAN COURTS BRING MORE JUSTICE TO HEALTH? (Alicia Ely Yamin & Sri Gloppen eds., 2011).

10. Robert M. Cover, *Foreword: Norms and Narratives*, 97 HARV. L. REV. 4, 4-5 (1983). *See* Andreas Follesdal, *Subsidiarity and the Global Order* at 207 in SUBSIDIARITY IN COMPARATIVE PERSPECTIVE (Augusto Zimmerman & Michelle Evans eds., 2014).

11. Carroza, *supra* note 3 at 57.

12. *Id.* at 57, 58.

13. *Id.*

14. *Id. See* Tomer Broude, *Keep Calm and Carry On: Martti Koskenniemi and the Fragmentation of International Law*, 27 TEMPLE INT'L & COMP. L. J. 279 (2013).

15. Andrew K. Woods, *A Behavioral Approach to Human Rights*, 51 HARV. INT'L L. J. 51 (2010).

16. *Id.*

17. *Id.* at 70, 71. It has been suggested that international law should be reconceived as a political right. Martti Koskenniemi, *The Fate of International Law: Between Technique and Politics*, 70 MOD. L. REV. 1, 29 (2007).

18. Carroza, *supra* note 3 at 58, 59.

19. *Id.*, at 59, 60. *See* Robin Perry, *Balancing Rights or Building Rights? Reconciling the Right to Use Customary Systems of Law with Competing Human Rights in Pursuit of Indigenous Sovereignty*, 24, HARV. HUM. RTS. J. 71 (2011). *See generally* VITTORIO COTESTA, GLOBAL SOCIETY AND HUMAN RIGHTS (2012).

20. Woods, *supra* note 15 at 70.

21. *Id. See* Eyal Benvenisti & George W. Downs, *The Emperor's New Clothes: Political Economy and the Fragmentation of International Law*, 60 STAN. L. REV. 595 (2007).

22. Woods, *supra* note 15 at 81, 87, 105. *See* Adam S. Chilton & Eric A. Posner, *The Influence of History on States' Compliance with Human Rights Obligations*, 56 VA. J. INT'L L. 211 (2016). *See also*, JACK GOLDSMITH, ERIC POSNER, THE LIMITS OF INTERNATIONAL LAW (2005).

23. MAITE SAN GIORGI, THE HUMAN RIGHT TO EQUAL ACCESS TO HEALTH CARE at 94, 95, Ch. 7 (2012). *See* Eric Heinze, *Even-Handedness and the Politics of Human Rights*, 21 HARV. HUM. RTS. J. 7 (2008); SANDRA FREDMAN, HUMAN RIGHTS TRANSFORMED: POSITIVE RIGHTS AND POSITIVE DUTIES at 92 *passim* (2008).

24. SAN GIORGI, *id.*

25. AHARON BARAK, HUMAN DIGNITY: THE CONSTITUTIONAL VALUE AND THE CONSTITUTIONAL RIGHT at 366 (2015).

26. *Id.*

27. *Id.*

28. *Id.*

29. *Id.*

30. *Id.*

31. *Id.* at 367.

32. GRUNDGESETZ (GG) [Constitution] Art. 1 (F.R.G.). *See* Christoph Goos, *Wurde des Menschen: Restoring Human Dignity in Post-Nazi Germany* at 79 in UNDERSTANDING HUMAN DIGNITY [hereinafter UNDERSTANDING DIGNITY].

33. Neomi Rao, *On the Use and Abuse of Dignity in Constitutional Law*, 14 COLUM. J. EUROPEAN L. 210, 219 (2008).

34. *Id.*

35. Doron Shultziner & Itai Ravinovici, *Human Dignity, Self-Worth and Humiliation: A Comparative Legal-Psychological Approach*, 18 PSYCHOLOGY, PUB. POL'Y & L. 105, 128 *passim* (2012).

36. *Id.* In 1980, human dignity was first used as a legal principle by the Supreme Court of Israel in Katalan v. Prison Authority, HCJ79/355, P.D. 34(3), 294 (1980).

37. BARAK, *supra* note 25 at 367.

38. *Id.*

39. 15

40. *See* JONAS CHRISTOFFERSON & MIKAEL RASK MADSEN, THE EUROPEAN COURT OF HUMAN RIGHTS BETWEEN LAW AND POLITICS (2011). *See also* THE EVOLUTION OF THE EUROPEAN CONVENTION ON HUMAN RIGHTS: FROM ITS INCEPTION TO THE CREATION OF A PERMANENT COURT OF HUMAN RIGHTS (Edward Bates ed., 2011). A review of some 600-odd judgments issued by the European Court of Human Rights where the word "dignity" was used by the Court as a tool for interpreting the European Convention on Human Rights, found that dignity was used almost exclusively to limited circumstances where physical or mental harm was found to have been inflicted on the applicant—primarily within the context of Article 3 of the Convention prohibiting torture and inhumane or degrading treatment or punishment. Shultziner & Ravinovici, *supra* note 35 at 124 *passim*.

41. *See* LAURENCE BURORGUE-LARSEN & AMAYA UBEDA DeTORRES, THE INTER-AMERICAN COURT OF HUMAN RIGHTS: CASE-LAW AND COMMENTARY (2011). *See also* Angel R. Oquendo, *The Politization of Human Rights: Within the Inter-American System and Beyond*, 50 N.Y.U. J. INT'L & POL. 1 (2017).

42. *Id.*

43. Shana Tabak, *Ambivalent Enforcement: International Humanitarian Law at Human Rights Tribunals*, 37 MICH. J. INT'L L. 661, 662 (2016). *See generally* Doron Shulziner, *Human Dignity in Judicial Decisions: Principles of Application and the Rule of Law*, 23 CARDOZO J. INT'L & COMP. L. 435 (2017).

44. Tabak, *id.*

45. *Id.*

46. *Id.*

47. *Id.* at 712. *See* Pierre Schmidt, *Access to Justice and International Organizations: The Case of Individual Victims of Human Rights Violations* (2017).

48. 2 JUDGE ANTONIO A. CANCADO TRINDADE, THE CONSTRUCTION OF A HUMANIZED INTERNATIONAL LAW 1770 *passim* (2015).

49. *Id.*, Vol. 1 at 125.

50. *Id.* at 148.
51. *Id.* at Ch. 3.
52. Shultziner & Rabinovici, *supra* note 35.
53. *Id.* at 30.
54. *Id.*
55. *Id.* at 31. *See* Csongor I. Nagy, *Do European Union Member States Have to Respect Human Rights? The Application of the European Union's Federal Bill of Rights to Member States*, 27 INDIANA INT'L & COMPARATIVE L. REV. 1 (2017).
56. *Supra* note 35 at 31. *See* Jean-Paul Costa, Ch. 22, *Human Dignity in the Jurisprudence of the European Court of Human Rights* at 393 in UNDERSTANDING DIGNITY, *supra* note 32.
57. Rao, *supra* note 33 at 255.
58. *Id.* at 227.
59. *Id.* at 223. *See generally* Harold H. Koh, *Why Do Nations Obey International Law?* 106 YALE L. J. 2599 (1997).
60. Rao, *supra* note 33 at 223.
61. *Id.*
62. *Id.*
63. *Id.* at 227.
64. *Id.* at 256.
65. *Id.*
66. *Id.* at 255.
67. *Id.*
68. *Id.* at 256.
69. *Id.*
70. Rao, *supra* note 33 at 235–36. *See* PETER HULSROJ, THE PRINCIPLE OF PROPORTIONALITY (2013).
71. *Id.*
72. *Id.*
73. *Id.*
74. Alec Stone Stewart & Judd Matthews, *Proportionality, Balancing and Global Constitutionalism* 47 COLUM. J. TRANSNATIONAL L. 73, 97 n. 53 (2008).
75. *Id.* at 90–95. *See* ROBERT ALEXY & JULIAN RIVERS, A THEORY OF CONSTITUTIONAL RIGHTS (2010).
76. Vicki C. Jackson, *Constitutional Law in an Age of Proportionality*, 124 YALE L. J. 3014 (2015).
77. *Id.* at 3106.
78. *Id.* at 3107.
79. *Id.* at 3108.
80. *Id.*
81. *Id.* at 3104–110.
82. *Id.* at 3104–121.
83. *Id.* at 3166–67.
84. *Id.* at 3110.

85. *Id.* at 3167. *See* AHARON BARAK, PROPORTIONALITY: CONSTITUTIONAL RIGHTS AND THEIR LIMITATIONS (2012).

86. Jackson, *id.*, at 3167. *See generally* Antonin Scalia, *The Rule of Law as a Law of Rules*, 56 U. CHI. L. REV. 1183 (1989).

87. Jackson, *supra* note 76 at 3167.

88. *Id. See* MICHAEL NEWTON & LARRY MAY, PROPORTIONALITY IN INTERNATIONAL LAW at 121–54 (2014).

89. Jackson, *supra* note 76 at 3168.

90. *Id.*

91. *Id.* at 3168–71.

92. *Id.* at 3167.

Chapter 6

Modern Formulations of Dignity: Clarifications and Calibrations

FOUR APPROACHES TO UNDERSTANDING

For dignity to have operational value in society—and, particularly, in America—a number of current proposals have been put forward. The first approach presents a Herculean task: namely, reshaping the administrative process in order to be more responsive to the pursuit and the protection of dignitary values. This is, indeed, a very ambitious and capacious theory that—presently—will be very difficult to implement. Its goal, however, is noble. Here, the argument is put forward that in order to preserve and enhance human dignity and self-respect, a decisional process is needed that facilitates a full level of participation by all participants.[1] It is through participation that a level of control is exerted over the complete "process of decision-making."[2] And, it is through participation that self-respect is promoted.[3] In order to meet its primary (if not sole) responsibility to "protect individual liberty,"[4] the state must, then, enable all citizens to engage fully in the full process of decision-making.[5] Yet, disparities in social-economic status,[6] as well as cognitive skills,[7] are often serious obstacles to achievement of this goal. Indeed, the promises of the liberal state to safeguard "privacy and equality" and promote "comprehensibility in the public decisional process," are thwarted because of these two handicaps.[8]

Constitutionalize the Administrative Process

It has been suggested that efforts must be made to constitutionalize the administrative process[9] in pursuit of the dignitary values of "autonomy, self-respect and equality."[10] The central issue to the dignitary theory proposed here, then, becomes determining whether the due process being challenged either sustains or diminishes individual dignity[11] and compromises procedural due process.[12]

Study the Components of Behaviorism

Three other approaches for clarifying dignity as a decisional or normative socio-legal standard in contemporary America are: 1) greater study of social or situational norms as components of behaviorism, 2) more extensive empirical research into what the personal consequences of a breach of human dignity are through victim assessments, and 3) advanced research into the components of social psychology and the necessary component of self-worth to the very notion of dignity.

Norms, such as dignity, develop from behaviorism.[13] Culture has the power to create or to undermine human rights norms.[14] The primary reason for this is that normative environments are composed of economic, social, cultural, civil, and political vectors of force.[15] In turn, these forces impact social conditions, which have the force of either enabling or disabling a multitude of behavioral life actions.[16]

Little attention has been given to "customary norms—the background patterns of both private and public expectation."[17] Indeed, the designers of human rights regimes have given insufficient attention to rich sources regarding "the role of social situations as distinct components of human behavior.[18] Without acknowledgment and utilization of behavioral research insights, regime designers are unable to create social situations or "normative universes" where human rights norms have social meaning.[19]

Utilize Dignity Narratives and Victims Tests

A third approach to calibrating human dignity is an effort to make it more functional as a norm or value calls for a better empirical understanding of what a breach of human dignity feels like for actual victims and the reasons that have caused it and, further, how future victimizations could be presented.[20] Inasmuch as dignity—within the context of human rights—is rather ephemeral, it has been suggested that dignity narratives, such as personal testaments and stories, might go for a better understanding of the contours of an offense of dignity or humiliation.[21] These, in turn, could form what might be styled a "victims test," which would allow an assessment to be made of the nature of the injuries suffered by the victims and the psychological and real life consequences (e.g., loss of employment, medical care) of these actions to their lives.[22] From these empirical tools, a "dignity-based judgment" could be made, which would study the whole process of victimization and evaluate the "degree of transformation" the established concepts of equality, autonomy, and sanctity of life were interpreted justly through the prism of human dignity in not only individual case of abuse but in general application.[23]

A subset to this notion of "victims tests" can already be seen in the Federal Crime Victim's Rights Act.[24] This legislation has proven—for some courts—to be a mechanism for broadening the rights of victims of crime.[25] Among the federal statutory rights protecting victims are some ten separate rights, with the eighth declaring that one has a "right to be treated with fairness and with respect for the victim's dignity and privacy."[26]

While most victim's rights laws—state and federal—allow a right of participation for the plaintiffs, a number of laws provide, explicitly, that victims have an "independent right to fair and dignified treatment."[27] And, in a number of laws addressing victim's rights, the concept or principle of dignity is often coupled with terms such as "fairness," "respect," and "privacy."[28] There is often a requirement in state laws that victims will be acknowledged and treated with "worthiness, honor, esteem, regard, and value."[29] Still, dignity is often limited by application of state courts as a background norm having interpretative value.[30]

Discern the Components of Self-Worth

A fourth theoretical approach also builds upon the use of empirical research by studying "the psychology of the self, specifically in the human need for maintaining positive self-worth."[31] It recognizes that norms—here dignity—develop from behaviorism,[32] and seeks to clarify the very notion of dignity by studying the consequences of indignity and victimization.[33] The history of the twentieth century is marked by one tragic feature: namely, that many of the most violent and destructive acts committed then are characterized today, properly, as humiliation and symbolic degradation.[34] Human rights—at their very core—are recognized in order to affirm not only the importance of the human character but the need for protection of "self-worth as a central factor of well-being."[35]

Significant research in social psychology during the second half of the twentieth century has shown impressive results regarding the capture and conceptualization of self-evaluation and a study of human needs.[36] A universal human need for "positive self-worth" or "positive self-esteem" has been established and shows clearly that when this status is achieved, "higher efficiency development (self-enhancement), happiness, satisfaction with life, better performances and persistence at tasks" are the clear results.[37]

The noble goal of this legal-psychological method is to transform and then operationalize the concept of dignity into a scientific concept capable of being measured and quantified for purposes of judicial decision-making.[38] The key attribute of this method is in specifying, within the human personality, shared mechanisms of self-evaluation and of worth—all with the idea of anchoring human dignity in statements that may be debated and elaborated upon through empirical grounds, which pertain to well-being.[39]

Although theoretical, this approach seeks to analyze the components of self-worth and proceed to determine whether a wrong has been committed that is either humiliating or harmful to one's sense of self-worth.[40] As observed, then, a working definition—or even a construct—will emerge that can be used as a tool for judicial decision-making. Translating empirical observations on dignity to a normative stipulation or "scientific concept" that positive self-worth should be of actual concern within a legal context is, however, indubitably problematic.[41]

PRINCIPLES, EMOTIONS, AND COMMON SENSE IN DECISION MAKING

At the center of efforts to formulate dignity as an operational value in society and particularly in the legal system that solidifies it, must come a recognition of the role that principles and emotions play in shaping a framework for principled decision-making.[42] Feelings are especially important when individuals or discrete issues arise that test the validity of a principle's application within the context of a given situation or norm of conduct.[43] It has been asserted that "the morally good person is not just principled, but also compassionate."[44] The morally good person, then, exhibits both "practical wisdom"[45] and "simple common sense[46] in preserving a patient's dignity or quality of life during medical care and at the end-state of life, itself.[47]

While compassion is experienced and evaluated subjectively,[48] it need not stigmatize a valid legal theory.[49] In *DeShaney v. Winnebago County Dept. of Social Services*,[50] Justice Blackmun addressed the importance of compassion in judicial analysis and interpretation by observing that "compassion in judicial analysis and interpretation by observing that "compassion need not be exiled from the province of judging."[51] He stated further that when a court removes "natural sympathy," it is unable to "recogniz[e] the facts of the case before it or the legal norms that should apply to those facts."[52]

Eschewing emotion as a dominant vector of force when seeking the truth in law,[53] Justice Oliver Wendell Holmes, Jr., urged that the reasoning behind a particular rule's adoption "ought to be of paramount importance."[54] And, when the reasons for structuring the rule have disappeared, it is improper to maintain the rule, simply due to "blind imitation of the past."[55]

The law should accord a greater "caring response" or a "sense of shared humanity"[56] in its interpretation and application. These values are essential to sustaining the rule of law.[57] Often, though, values are challenged or perceived as being in conflict with "moralistic abstractions about liberty, equality, and dignity."[58]

Unquestionably, health care decisions concerning the maintenance of life and the hastening of death often pose complicated moral questions that are anchored in normative reasoning, which may soon become irrelevant because of changing contemporary values.[59] If moral reasoning is found to be ambiguous or ineffectual, courts will rely on "moral intuitions," or "assumptions about intrinsic normative order" found implicitly "in the natural course of life."[60] Analytical frameworks of this nature invite conflict because of non-verifiable subjective values—this, because determining normative assumptions that animate moral judgments is very difficult if not indiscernible.[61]

In order to add greater precision to their analyses, courts can choose to embrace the philosophy of Holmes, which prizes logic over experience.[62] By adhering to legal formalism, moral judgments are avoided altogether.[63] This is largely because there is an awareness that it is very difficult to safeguard and sustain social solidarity if purely emotional values are given weight during the processes of judicial decision-making.[64] If formalism is rejected, however, judicial deference can be given to "tradition and convention"[65] as an imperfect means for discerning moral convictions or discovering shared ones.[66]

The best model of judicial decision-making achieves a balance between logical reasoning and "critical morality."[67] As such, the courts must endeavor to apply a situation ethic rather than an unyielding and rigid normative standard,[68] and then proceed to acknowledge love or agape as the controlling moral principle in all judicial decision-making. Stated otherwise, the judiciary should seek to interpret evolving social values while guided by compassion or humaneness.[69] These values and conditions will necessarily change with the facts of each case and, so too, will the pertinence of compassion and humaneness. The ultimate goal of judicial decision-making should be a "practical realization of the rule of law."[70]

NOTES

1. Jerry L. Mashaw, *Administrative Due Process: The Question of a Dignitary Theory*, 61 BOSTON U. L. REV. 885, 866 (1981).
2. *Id.* at 903.
3. *Id.*
4. ROBERT NOZICK, ANARCHY, STATE AND UTOPIA 10–25, 118 (1974).
5. Mashaw, *supra* note 1 at 903.
6. *See* Jeanne S. Zaino, *Self-Respect and Rawlsian Justice*, 60 J. POLITICS 737 (1998). *See also*, JOHN RAWLS, A THEORY OF JUSTICE (1971) (where he

constructs a society that may retain large disparities in socio-economic status for indeterminate periods of time, but then posits these inequalities will not cause citizens to experience any diminishment in worth because self-respect is related to legally prescribed rights and liberties and not socio-economic status). *Id.* at 440.

7. *See* CHARLES MURRAY, THE BELL CURVE (1994).

8. Mashaw, *supra* note 1 at 922.

9. *Id.* at 929.

10. *Id.* at 910.

11. *Id.* at 894.

12. *See* Mary M. Giannini, *The Procreative Power of Dignity: Dignity's Evolution in the Victim's Rights Movement*, 9 DREXEL L. REV. 43, 48 (2016) (analyzing Mashaw's efforts to equate dignity with due process).

13. Andrew K. Woods, *A Behavioral Approach to Human Rights*, 51 HARV. INT'L. L. J. 51 (2010).

14. *Id.* at 105.

15. *Id.* at 70–81.

16. *Id.* at 70–87, 112.

17. *Id.* at 107.

18. *Id.* at 111.

19. *Id.* at 106, 111.

20. Catherine Dupre, Ch. 5, Constructing The Meaning Of Dignity: Four Questions at 113 in UNDERSTANDING HUMAN DIGNITY at 113 (Christopher McCrudden ed., 2013).

21. *Id.*

22. *Id.*

23. *Id.* at 120.

24. 18 U.S.C. s3371 (2012).

25. Giannini, *supra* note 12 at 92 *passim.*

26. *Id.* at 72.

27. *Id.* 66.

28. *Id.*

29. *Id.* at 73.

30. *Id.* at 76.

31. Doron Shultziner & Itai Rabinovici, *Human Dignity, Self-Worth and Humiliation: A Comparative Legal-Psychological Approach*, 18 PSYCHOLOGY, PUB. POL'Y & L. 105, 125 *passim. See* HUMAN DIGNITY: ESTABLISHING WORTH AND SELF-WORTH (Edward Sieth & Judy McGregor eds., 2017).

32. Woods, *supra* note 13.

33. Shultziner & Rabinovici, *supra* note 31.

34. *See* JONATHAN GLOVER, HUMANITY: A MORAL HISTORY OF THE TWENTIETH CENTURY (1999).

35. Shultziner & Itai Rabinovici, *supra* note 31 at 108 *passim.*

36. *Id.* at 109 *passim.*

37. *Id.* at 107 *passim. See generally* DIGNITY, CHARACTER, AND SELF-RESPECT (Robert S. Dillon ed., 1998).

38. Shultziner & Rabinovici, *supra* note 31 at 135–37.
39. *Id.* at 113 *passim.*
40. *Id.* at 135–37.
41. *Id.* at 112–13.
42. George P. Smith, II, *Refractory Pain, Existential Suffering, and Palliative Care: Releasing an Unbearable Lightness of Being*, 20 CORNELL J. L. & PUB. POL'Y 469, at 521 (2011).
43. FIONA RANDALL & ROBIN S. DOWNIE, PALLIATIVE CARE ETHICS: A GOOD COMPANION 12–13 (1996).
44. *Id.* at 13.
45. *Id.* at 24.
46. *Id.* at 73.
47. *Id.* at 71.
48. Benjamin Zipursky, *DeShaney and the Jurisprudence of Compassion*, 65 N.Y.U.L. REV. 1001 (1990).
49. *Id.* at 1142.
50. *DeShaney v. Winnebago County Dept. of Social Services*, 489 U.S. 189 (1988).
51. 489 U.S. at 213 (Blackmun, J. dissenting).
52. *Id.* at 213.
53. THE ESSENTIAL HOLMES: SELECTIONS FROM THE LETTERS, SPEECHES, JUDICIAL OPINIONS, AND OTHER WRITINGS OF OLIVER WENDELL HOLMES, JR. 119 (Richard A. Posner ed., 1992).
54. Oliver Wendell Holmes, Jr., *The Path of The Law*, 10 HARV. L. REV. 457 (1987); *see* RICHARD A. POSNER, LAW, PRAGMATISM AND DEMOCRACY 107 (2003) (arguing that ordinary people have little interest in complex policies and limited intellectual depth—with half of the population with IQs of below 100).
55. Holmes, *id.*
56. *Id.* at 457.
57. Neil S. Siegel, *The Virtue of Judicial Statesmanship*, 86 TEX. L. REV. 961, 971 (2008).
58. *Id.* at 1030.
59. Steven D. Smith, *De-Moralized: Glucksberg in the Malaise*, 106 MICH. L. REV. 1571, 1589 (2008).
60. *See id.* at 1589–90.
61. *See id.* at 1589.
62. *See generally* Holmes, *supra* note 54 (a collection of various writings from the distinguished Supreme Court Justice that impart his philosophy on jurisprudence).
63. Smith, *supra* note 59, at 1590.
64. *See generally* Cass R. Sunstein, *Due Process Traditionalism*, 106 MICH. L. REV. 1543 (2008) (explaining arguments on behalf due process traditionalism and ultimately concluding that these arguments provide a tenuous defense of judicial decision-making); *see also* WILLIAM F. SULLIVAN, EYE OF THE HEART: KNOWING THE HUMAN GOOD IN THE EUTHANASIA DEBATE 27–58 (2005).
65. Smith, *supra* note 59, at 1590.

66. *Id.*

67. *Id.* Judge Richard Posner suggests that by employing a type of reasoning termed, "cultural cognition," which is considered "a valid[,] though flawed[,] sense of knowledge," a judge is allowed to consider his personal vision of those policies important to him in order to advance his model of a good society. *Id.* "The personal, the emotional and the intuitive" are factors used in judicial-making—with the intuitive being a real factor in appellate review. RICHARD A. POSNER, *supra* note 54, at 116, 117.

68. *See* JOHN FLETCHER, SITUATION ETHICS: THE NEW MORALITY (1966) (arguing for a new approach to ethics grounded in love and married to an objective rationale of utility). *See generally* HARRY G. FRANKFORT, THE REASONS OF LOVE (2004).

69. Siegel, *supra* note 57, at 981.

70. *Id.* at 979; *see generally* George P. Smith, II, *Judicial Decisionmaking in the Age of Biotechnology*, 13 NOTRE DAME J. L. ETHICS & PUB. POL'Y 93 (1999) (calling for courts to consider the modern refinements of biotechnology in conjunction with social policy in shaping judicial decisions regarding bioethics).

Chapter 7

Advancing Global Frameworks toward a New Social Order

THE UNITED NATIONS

Pivotal to a global initiative to structure a framework in order to advance a new human rights constitutionalism[1] are three instruments: the Universal Declaration on Human Genome and Human Rights[2] of 1998, the 2003 International Declaration on Human Genetic Data,[3] and the Universal Bioethics Declaration of 2005.[4] In addition to these Declarations, the Universal Declaration of Human Rights,[5] the International Covenant on Civil and Political Rights,[6] and the International Covenant on Economic, Cultural, and Social Rights[7] set forth working principles and impose obligations that bear a direct, rather than a tangential, relationship to normative medical ethics.[8]

Human rights, bioethics, and medical ethics are linked together, inextricably, by provisions in these United Nations Declarations, which require respect for human dignity and equality, the right to life, the realization of a standard of living that promotes health and assures medical care, together with the right to be free from inhumane and degrading treatment.[9] Respect for human dignity and for equality are also to be found within the Convention on the Rights of the Child.[10] This Convention presents an unequivocal statement of commitment from subscribing states and their institutions, to protect—specifically—a child's best interests (economic, social, and cultural) as derived directly from the family unit[11] and thereby safeguard both children and their families.[12]

The Universal Declaration on Bioethics and Human Rights was adopted on October 19, 2005, by the member states of UNESCO.[13] The Declaration in Article 1 enunciates a Principle of Social Responsibility, which directs decisions and practice in science and technology advance "the common good" by providing "access to adequate nutrition and water," eliminating the marginalization of persons, and reducing poverty and illiteracy.[14] Article 15 strengthens the very notion of social responsibility by directing the benefits of scientific research to advance, among other interests, "access to quality health care" and "support for health services."[15]

Article 23 of the Bioethics and Human Rights Declaration underscores state responsibilities to safeguard public health standards by using proportionate measures designed to not only accord respect for "human dignity, human rights, and fundamental freedoms," but they be undertaken pro-actively when "threats of serious irreversible damage to public health or human welfare" exist.[16] The Declaration can be properly seen, then, as a creative effort to recognize, and thus validate, an inextricable symbiotic relationship between human dignity and human rights with "access" to health care. Indeed, in this regard, if not accepted as an independent human right, dignity must be accepted as, at a minimum, an integral part of the human right to health care.

The European Convention on Human Rights and Biomedicine—although of marginal impact because of its limited ratification—should none the less be recognized as a creative illustration of linkage with bioethics, medical ethics, and the norms of international human rights.[17] This linkage is found through policies regulating equitable access to healthcare and informed consent, together with restrictions on the uses of the human genome and other regulations on scientific research.[18]

Although all of these U.N. Conventions and Declarations are significant in their effect to structure an international policy framework for this New Age of Biotechnology, one central flaw to their permanence and their effectiveness exists: that is, the fact that principles, covenants, statutes, protocols, declarations, and conventions bind *only* states that either accede or ratify them.[19]

The standards of progressivity shape any and all political efforts to design and then enforce a right to health as either a social, political, or a cultural right.[20] This fragile—if not fatally flawed enforcement—mechanism grants an immunity to all states from human rights violations *so long as* they present evidence of their progressive (or at least measurable) actions toward the realization of human rights.[21]

The U.N.'s Economic and Social Council (ECOSOC) acts as a strong counter influence to mediate the standards of progressivity's negative impact realizing human rights.[22] As part of an action plan for promoting and realizing human rights put forward by the Committee on Economic, Social, and Cultural Rights, core minimum obligations are imposed on all State parties who have ratified the Covenant on Economic, Social, and Cultural Rights and the Covenant on Civil and Political Rights—covenants that must be met regardless of any modifications granted under the standards.[23]

Economic self-interest and political survival determine, in the final analysis and application, the level of both the recognition and the enforcement of health-care protections and the extent to which they are accepted or rejected as an integral part of social, cultural, political, or human rights. A strong civil society, operating freely, is essential in order to secure sustainable human rights nationally.[24]

SHAPING AN EQUITABLE TEMPLATE

Hugo Grotius, in his 1625 classic *De Jure Belli ac Pacis Libri Tres*, or, *The Law of War and Peace*,[25] found that Aristotle championed the notion that all treaties should be interpreted using principles of equity.[26] In international law, equity is recognized as "a non-consensual source" used either to supplement or modify conventional rules and customary usages of international law.[27] Early nineteenth- and twentieth-century arbitration treaties provided explicitly for the application of principles of equity to be applied in international law in interpreting treaties.[28] Equity has always been seen as a form of judicial discretion,[29] as well as a form of distributive justice[30]—especially, modernly, as viewed with issues of maritime delimitations and the law of the sea.[31]

The "universal law of society" is presumed to include customary law.[32] As a result of this recognition, international lawyers are in general agreement that it is appropriate and—indeed proper—for outreach to be made beyond treaties and custom and to general principles of law, natural law, and to equity[33] in order to find and to establish and protect the parameters of the bases of his universal law.[34]

Interestingly, equitable principles, which form a part of the corpus of international law, are seen as separate—in application—from adjudicating cases *ex aequo et bono* (or, what is good and fair).[35] Seen as a vital integrative force within international law, equity is not restricted in its application and utilizes as the principle of *ex aequo et bono*. Specifically, under Article 38 of the Permanent Court of International Justice, the power of the Court to use *ex aequo et bono* is granted to the court "if the parties agree thereto."[36] Even with these distinctions between equitable principles and the use of *ex aequo et bono*, their very acknowledgment alone goes far to establish a template—if not a construct for evidencing and applying the transnational standard of equity.

Equity is understood popularly, as signifying "natural justice or whatever is right and just as between man and man."[37] The antecedents of equity are acknowledged as "a system of jurisprudence which originated and developed outside the common law writs of England to supply to suitors remedial relief not obtainable in the common law courts."[38]

It is clear from judicial practice that the proper interpretation of Article 38 of the Permanent Court of International Justice does not "depend on a pre-supposed hierarchical arrangement of sources of law."[39] Because of this liberal posture, equity has long been recognized as a general principle of interpretation.[40] International Law judges, through *lex judicia* or judicial reasoning, apply equity as a cognizable source of law.[41]

Rather, than have equity castigated conceptually for being subject to wide discretionary abuse, it is more productive to "distinguish the proper recourse to equity from the improper."[42] Ideally, this process will then yield a result akin to Aristotle's Golden Mean.[43] In the *Nicomachean Ethics*,[44] Aristotle finds that every action and choice aims "at some good."[45] The Golden Mean is a characterization of virtue.[46] It presents a standard of ethical behavior and is attained after a balance or "mean" between thinking and acting or between two vices—one of excess and the other of deficiency—is reached.[47] Interpreting equity's goal as consistent with and complimentary to Aristotle's Mean results in equity being conceived properly as "the artful and judicially determined balance between reason and rule."[48]

Although equity originally protected only property rather than personal or individual rights,[49] the modern trend has been to extend equitable relief to protect personal rights "that are existent and judicially cognizable"[50]—and especially the ever-strengthening rights to privacy.[51] Equally, equity has shown its outreach to protect civil rights.[52] Arguably, the "right" to protect well-being is within the zone of privacy and protectable as a civil right. The inherent hope (and promise) of equity then, is that it "corrects inequalities."[53]

Security, human dignity, well-being, compassion, and humanism are values that the courts must—domestically and internationally—secure through simply applying equity to judicial decision-making, which for purposes of analysis in this book, apply to managing futile medical conditions at the end-stage of life in such a manner to assure whatever degree of kindness and compassion that can be given under the facts of any given situation.

JUS COGENS NORMS AND *ERGA OMNES* OBLIGATIONS

Recognized as a concept of natural law, *jus cogens* (or compelling law) is a preemptory norm accepted as a basic principle of international law[54] and accepted by the international community of states as a norm that generates obligations *erga omnes*.[55] These obligations, in turn, are seen as state-based and are owed to the international community as a whole.[56] The overlap between *jus cogens* norms and *erga omnes* obligations continue to be contentious with no definitive resolution presently.[57]

This notion of *jus cogens* was, no doubt, inspired by international scholars in the sixteenth and in the seventeenth centuries and especially Christian Wolff who, in 1749, postulated a theory of *civitas maxima* (or supreme state) as the foundation for a voluntary law of nations.[58] For Wolff, a *civitas maxima* was, then, a coalition or confederation of diverse social, ethic and/or cultural groups bound together by common legal, moral, and cultural ties.[59] Other scholars have proceeded to posit theoretical foundations of a world order based on a priority of values reflecting a hierarchy of norms.[60] As projections of the individual and collective conscience, peremptory human rights norms, then, are seen as strong, collective beliefs.[61]

Historically and contemporaneously, no exhaustive line of pre-emptory norms has been drawn.[62] Yet, an almost intrinsic relationship between *jus cogens* and human rights can be found. Indeed, the vast majority of case law where *jus cogens* has been invoked is concerned with both the protection and the violation of human rights.[63] Thus, there can be no debate that human rights norms have attained full pre-emptory status.[64]

Because of its all-encompassing reach, *jus cogens* cannot be limited to the law of treaties, anchored by the Vienna Convention on the Law of Treaties, which entered into force in 1980.[65] Rather, there remains a fundamental international responsibility—enforced juridically—to embrace *jus cogens* as an acknowledgment of the very international community as a whole and as a vital source of a new *jus gentium* or international law for humankind.[66]

NOTES

1. *See* George P. Smith, II, HUMAN RIGHTS AND BIOMEDICINE (2000). It has been suggested that legal pluralism be acknowledged as an alternative to constitutionalism. Martti Koskenniemi, *The Fate of International Law: Between Technique and Politics*, 70 MOD. L. REV. 1, 29 (2007).
2. UNESCO, Final Report, BIO-97 CONF 201/9 C22-25 (July, 1997).
3. UNESCO 32/C Res 22 (16 October 2003). *See* www.unesco.org/new/en/social-and-humane-sciences/themes/bioethics/bioethics-and/humanrights.
4. SHS/EST/CIB-EXTR/05/Conf.202/2 (Feb. 9, 2005). *See* www.unesco.org/new/en/social-and-humane-sciences/themes/bioethics/bioethics-and/humanrights. *As well*, the 1978 Declaration of Alma-Ata must be listed as a foundational source for recognizing primary health care as fundamental to the very ideal of attaining the universal goal of basic health care for all. *See* BENJAMIN M. MEIR, THE HIGHEST ATTAINTABLE STANDARD: THE WORLD HEALTH ORGANIZATION, GLOBAL HEALTH GOVERNANCE AND THE CONTENTIOUS POLITICS OF HUMAN RIGHTS (2011).
5. U.N. G.A. Res. 217A, U.N. Doc. A/810, at 71 (1948). *See* Appendix B, *infra*.

6. 16 December 1966, 933 UNTS 3. The United States signed the Convention in 1977 and it was ratified by the Senate in 1992 with 5 reservations, 5 understandings, and 4 declarations. It entered into force also in 1992. *See* Appendix D, *infra*.

7. 16 December 1966, 999 UNTS 171 (the United States is a party, subject to several reservations, understandings, and declarations). Although signed, the Covenant has not been ratified by the Senate. *See* Appendix C, *infra*. Collectively, these three dignitarian instruments are seen as the International Bill of Rights. STEPHEN JAMES, UNIVERSAL RIGHTS 8 (2007).

8. George P. Smith, II, *Human Rights and Bioethics: Formulating a Universal Right to Health Care or Health Care Protection?* 38 VANDERBILT TRANSNAT'L L. J. 1295 (2005).

9. *Id. See generally* LOUIS HENKIN, THE RIGHTS OF MAN TODAY, Ch. 2 (1978). Interestingly, the U.S. Constitution—because it was not regarded as a Charter of rights and liberties, but rather a blueprint of government—did not provide any specific formulae of rights. *See* Appendix F, *infra*, for a listing by the Office of the United Nations High Commissioner for Human Rights of approximately 100 universal instruments which advance and protect human rights.

10. Art. 3, Nov. 20, 1989, 1577 U.N.T.S. 3.

11. *Id.*, at Preamble.

12. *Id.*, Arts. 2–4. *See* Peggy Cooper Davis, *Little Citizens and Their Families*, 43 FORDHAM URB. L. J. 1009 (2016). *See also* Jane M. Spinck, *Dignity Rights: A Response to Peggy Cooper Davis' Little Citizens and Their Families*, 43 FORDHAM URB. L. J. 1221 (2016).

13. *See* UNESCO FINAL REPORT, BIO-97 Conf 201/9 C22-25 (July, 1997) and Appendix E, *infra*. *See also* Michael D. Kirby, *Human Rights: The Universal Declaration of Human Rights* and UNESCO Declaration on Bioethics and Human Rights, 25 J. CONTEMP. HEALTH L. & POL'Y 309 (2009).

14. *Id.*

15. *Id.*

16. *Id.*

17. Thomas Faunce, *Will Human Rights Subsume Medical Ethics? Intersections in the UNESCO Universal Bioethics Declarations*, 31 J. MED. ETHICS 173 (2004).

18. *Id.*

19. Smith, *supra* note 8. *See* Appendix E, *infra*.

20. THERESE MURPHY, HEALTH AND HUMAN RIGHTS at 41–42 (2013).

21. HENRY J. STEINER & PHILIP ALSTON, INTERNATIONAL HUMAN RIGHTS IN CONTEXT: LAWS, POLITICS, MORALS (192–194 [1996]). A procedure framed as the Universal Periodic Review, conducted by the United Nation's Intergovernmental Human Rights Council every five years of all member states of the U.N., is another noble effect to assess, monitor, and implement individual state policies designed to promote global health. Regrettably, economic and social conditions often militate against strong recommendations designed to maintain standards which allow for practical applications of sound public health actions. Jane K. Cowan & Julie Billard, *Between Learning and Schooling: The Politics of Human Rights Monitoring at the Universal Periodic Review*, 36 THIRD WORLD QUARTERLY 1175 (2015).

See CATHERINE DUPREE, THE AGE OF DIGNITY: HUMAN RIGHTS AND CONSTITUTIONALISM (2015).

22. HOLGER HESTERMEYER, HUMAN RIGHTS AND THE WTO (2007). *See* Roberto Adorno, *Human Dignity and Human Rights as a Common Ground for Global Bioethics*, 34 J. MED. & PHIL. 225 (2009).

23. HESTERMEYER, *id.*, at 111. *See generally* LOCAL ENGAGEMENT WITH INTERNATIONAL ECONOMIC LAW AND HUMAN RIGHTS (Ljiljana Biukovic & Pitman B. Potter eds., 2017).

24. George P. Smith, II, *Access to Health Care: Economic, Medical, Ethical and Socio-Legal Challenges* at Ch. 20, in AUTONOMY AND HUMAN RIGHTS AND HEALTH CARE (D. N. Weisstub & G. D. Pinto eds., 2008). *See* Appendix E, *infra*. *See also*, Cowan & Billard, *supra* note 21.

25. *See generally* HUGO GROTIUS, THE LAW OF WAR AND PEACE (Francis W. Kelsey trans., 1925) (discussing how treaties should be interpreted using notions of equity).

26. MARK W. JANIS, AN INTRODUCTION TO INTERNATIONAL LAW at 74–75 (3rd ed., 1999).

27. *Id.* at 54.

28. *Id.* at 52.

29. Three forms of equity are recognized: Equity *intra legem* (within the law) applicable to eases so as to achieve the law's intent "without exceeding the law's formal language." Equity *praeter legem*, seen as a bold application by a judge to essentially "fill in gaps and supplant the law with equitable rules necessary to decide" an instant case. And, equity *contra legem*, seen as the most contentious of equitable glosses, because it disregards any "pertinent" law of a case with the purpose of achieving an equitable result "despite the law's explicit injunction." JANIS, *id.* at 57.

30. *Id.* at 52.

31. *Id.* at 59, 65. *See* KEMAL BASTAR, THE CONCEPT OF THE COMMON HERITAGE OF MANKIND IN INTERNATIONAL LAW (1998).

32. *U.S. v. Smith*, 18 U.S. (5 Wheaton) 153, 161 (1820).

33. *See supra* note 29 for the three types of equity.

34. JANIS, *supra* note 26.

35. *Netherlands v. Belgium* (1937), Judge Hudson's Opinion, 1937 P.C.I.J. Reports, sec. A/B, no. 70, at 73, 76.

36. Statute of the International Court of Justice, art. 38 (2), as annexed to the Charter of the United Nations, 59 Stat. 1055, T.S. No. 993.

37. *See also* WILLIAM Q. DeFUNIAK, HANDBOOK ON MODERN EQUITY Ch. 1 (2nd ed., 1956).

38. *Id.* at 2.

39. CHRISTOPHER R. ROSSI, EQUITY AND INTERNATIONAL LAW 250 (1999).

40. *Id.* at 83.

41. *Id.* at 250.

42. *Id.* at 255.

43. *Id.* at 252.

44. Aristotle, NICHOMACHEAN ETHICS (Martin Osterwald trans., 1962).
45. *Id.* at 3.
46. *Id.* at 43.
47. *Id.*
48. ROSSI, *supra* note 39 at 252.
49. DeFUNIAK, *supra* note 37 at 10.
50. *Id.* at 124–31.
51. *Id.* at 131.
52. *Id.* at 140.
53. MOHAMMED BEDAJAOUI, TOWARDS A NEW INTERNATIONAL ECONOMIC ORDER 127 (1979).
54. ALEXANDER ORAKHELASHVILI, PEREMPTORY NORMS IN INTERNATIONAL LAW (2006). *See* THE FUNDAMENTAL RULES OF INTERNATIONAL LEGAL ORDER: *JUS COGENS* AND *ERGA OMNES* at Ch. 3 (Christian Tomuschat & Jean-Marc Thouvenin eds., 2006).
55. CHRISTIAN J. TAMS, ENFORCING OBLIGATIONS *ERGA OMNES* IN INTERNATIONAL LAW (2005).
56. *Id. See* Paolo Picone, *The Distinction between Jus Cogens and Obligations Erga Omnes* at Ch. 24 in THE LAW OF TREATIES BEYOND THE VIENNA CONVENTION (Enzo Cannizzaro ed., 2011). *See also* 1 JUDGE ANTONIO A. CANCADO TRINDADE, THE CONSTRUCTION OF A HUMANIZED INTERNATIONAL LAW at 339 (2015).
57. *Id.*
58. Nicholas G. Onuf, *Civitas Maxima: Wolff, Vattel and the Fate of Republicanism*, 88 AM. J. INT'L L. 280 (1994).
59. *Id.*
60. Andrea Bianchi, *Human Rights and the Use of Jus Cogens*, 10 EUROPEAN J. INT'L L. 491, 493–94 (2009).
61. *Id. See* MARK W. JANIS, *supra* note 26 at 53–66 (submitting that human dignity and well-being should be acknowledged as a part of *jus cogens* and thus a fundamental pre-emptory norm the violation of which invalidates rules consented to by states in treaties or accepted custom).
62. BIANCHI, *supra* note 60, *id.*
63. *Id.* at 492.
64. TRINDADE, *supra* note 56 at 494. *See* JANIS, *supra* note 26. *See also* PATRICK CAPPS, HUMAN DIGNITY AND THE FOUNDATIONS OF INTERNATIONAL LAW (2009).
65. 1 TRINDADE, *supra* note 56 at 148, 444.
66. *Id.* at 158–59. *See* JUDGE ANTONIO A. CANCADO TRINDADE, INTERNATIONAL LAW FOR HUMANKIND; TOWARDS A NEW "*JUS GENTIUM*" (2nd ed., 2010). *See also* Robin Perry, *Balancing Rights or Building Rights? Reconciling the Right to Use Customary Systems of Law with Competing Human Rights in Pursuit of Indigenous Sovereignty*, 24 HARV. HUM. RTS. J. 71 (2011).

Conclusions

As a concept, principle, normative standard, or value, human dignity may be viewed correctly as predating human rights—this, because human rights are, in contemporary society, seen as "judicial concretization," of but a generalized notion of human dignity.[1] Owing to the capacious nature of human rights, clarity of application or human dignity as a normative standard is understandably elusive. Indeed, attempting to define limits to dignity is especially perplexing since respecting dignity not only implies respect for individual autonomy but "the right to everyone not to be devalued as a human being" or be degraded and humiliated.[2] To respect human dignity is to "respect an individual's standing as being possessed of intrinsic worth."[3]

Standing alone, the virtue of dignity should not be acknowledged as being single and distinct from, for example, courage. Rather, dignity should be understood as "a collection of loosely related traits like self-respect, self-control, and self-discipline."[4] The very taxonomy of human dignity, then, is set within the "context of respect for persons and the value of autonomy."[5] Indeed, human dignity may be viewed correctly as the threshold of, or catalyst for, a morality of equal respect; a respect which can be asserted solely by virtue of the status one has as a citizen living in a democratic society and not by virtue of attained social status or by personal achievement[6]—but, rather, as a consequence of a shared or "common humanity."[7] Preserving self-worth requires the felt need to protect against insult and humiliation[8]; for, having a sense of self-worth means that one "matters" in the social order.[9] Without this sense, there is no dignity.[10]

In 1986, Justice William J. Brennan of the U.S. Supreme Court opined that "a comprehensive definition of the constitutional idea and the demands of human dignity will never cease to evolve."[11] Others express hope that this evolvement will yield a judicial recognition of human dignity as both a value and a constitutional right.[12] A third, less sanguine opinion holds that because of the entrenchment of dignity in moral discourse, dignity will continue to be used "as a cloak behind which interested parties seek to impose moral prescriptions that lack the legitimacy of a popular mandate."[13]

What remains indisputable is the fact that all of the international instruments on human rights, at one level or other, have human dignity as their *raison d'etre* and end goal.[14] Consequently, the optimum value of maximizing human dignity is codified, then, when laws and policies that administer justice are guided by the central, modern virtue of human dignity.[15] If human dignity is acknowledged as the ultimate value, or even as a foundational value, it assumes "the function of a social ideal rather than that of a value having any direct utility."[16]

It has been suggested, as seen, that—in reality—because of the ambiguities in definition and application, the essential worth of human dignity as a concept is "limited,"[17] problematic, and open to question.[18] Logical as these concerns are, human dignity must nonetheless be evaluated and applied—if not as a catalyst for normative conduct, then as a "common ground for moral understanding"[19] a tool for consensus morality,[20] or perhaps a template for safeguarding international equity.[21]

It is important to remember that the very ends of medicine are devoted to preserving human dignity and preventing indignity.[22] It remains for the physician to recognize a duty of beneficence to safeguard the patient from losing dignity and thereby despairing[23] and be ever mindful that, independent of bodily pain—extreme abasement and humiliation, loss of hope and demoralization, may result in acute existential pain and that this must be dealt with in an appropriate manner.[24]

One of the inherent weaknesses of the rule of law is its all too frequent efforts to distance itself from human experience.[25] In order to compensate or even remediate this situation, it has been urged that sympathy and compassion be integrated into contemporary law.[26] A contemporary and principled rule of law, thus, needs notions of decency, dignity, and compassion within its very sinews.[27] Others have called for the law to be empathetic or to incorporate concepts of love, altruism and sympathy.[28]

While principles provide the foundational framework for standards of normative conduct, feelings are important when individual or *micro* issues arise, which, in turn, test the extent to which principles are valid in their application within the context of a given or norm of conduct.[29] It is asserted that "the morally good person is not just principled, but also compassionate."[30] That person, additionally, not only exhibits "practical wisdom" but, as well, "common sense" in assuring patient dignity or quality of life is preserved throughout the ritual of dying.[31]

At the end-stage of life, health care management decision-making should be guided, ideally, by a situation ethic that is shaped by, not only common sense, but by beneficence, compassion, and love,[32] and which seeks to assure dignity in dying. Consistent with the principle of medical futility, physicians should be emboldened to take reasonable and sound professional measures to alleviate pain and existential suffering.[33] When deemed appropriate to a particular case, and consistent with patient values and life experiences—deep or palliative sedation should, for example, be seen as not only efficacious but compassionate care that preserves human dignity.[34]

The importance of preserving human dignity at the end-of-life should, ideally, be recognized as a human right.[35] Imprecise as the term is and conditioned, as such, by economic, cultural, social and political forces with each member state of the United Nations,[36] having human dignity nonetheless codified in international policy documents is significant.[37] Although admittedly symbolic, the importance of human dignity alternatively, as a normative catalyst for ongoing dialogue and for implementation in action programs for the attainment and safeguarding of human rights by the United Nations ECOSOC and the Committee on Economic, Social and Cultural Rights, cannot be overstated. The eloquent words in the Preamble to the U.N. Charter, which came into force in 1945, remain—today—a clarion call to establish and secure "the dignity and the worth of the human person"[38] by recognizing the right to die with dignity as an inviolable human right—for, the right to dignity reflects, most appropriately, more than any other right can or does, the very essence of what being a human being means.[39] Dignity should be viewed rightly as nothing less than "an expression of the unity of mankind" and of a common humanity.[40]

Planning end-of-life management decisions or death induction plans within the framework of human rights protections, is as important for individuals as it is for the democratic society in which they live. The reason for this linkage is that these decisions are seen simply as "important in lives."[41] Even though no right to die is recognized domestically and internationally, the very "right to life, to dignity, and self-determination apply throughout" one's life—and especially so at its end-stage and conclusion.[42] In the final analysis, "the fundamental questions in law and ethics will be shaped by what we think it means to be human and what we understand to be ethical obligations owed to the human person,"[43] as well as whether human dignity can be realized as the fundamental vector of force in shaping standards of social justice.[44] As Mary Ellen Caldwell has stated so eloquently, "Human dignity—an international human right to well-being, to respect and deference, simply because we are human—seems wholly dependent upon our willing it to be so and our collective acceptance of some of the somber consequences in the exercise of that will."[45]

NOTES

1. Dietrich Ritschl, *Can Ethical Maxims Be Derived from Theological Concepts of Human Dignity* in CONCEPT OF HUMAN DIGNITY, in THE CONCEPT OF HUMAN DIGNITY IN HUMAN RIGHTS DISCOURSE at 87, 92 (David Kretzmer & Eckart Klein eds., 2002) [hereinafter CONCEPT OF HUMAN DIGNITY].

2. Arthur Chaskalson, *Comparative Constitutional Perspectives: Human Dignity as a Constitutional Value* in CONCEPT OF HUMAN DIGNITY, *id.* at 133, 134.

3. J. M. Bernstein, TORTURE AND DIGNITY: AN ESSAY ON MORAL INJURY at 311 (2015). Lack of self-respect deprives all activities of meaning by undermining the very point of pursing them (agreeing with John Rawls). *Id.* at 305.

4. Michael Meyer, *Dignity as a Modern Value* in CONCEPT OF HUMAN DIGNITY, *supra* note 1 at 195, 197, 202–05. *See* MATHIAS LUTZ-BACHMANN, HUMAN RIGHTS, HUMAN DIGNITY, AND COSMOPOLITAN IDEALS (2013).

5. David N. Weisstub, *Honor, Dignity and The Framing of Multicultural Values* in CONCEPT OF HUMAN DIGNITY, *supra* note 1 at 269. *See generally* C. Ben Mitchell, *The Audacity of The Imago Dei*, in IMAGO DEI: HUMAN DIGNITY IN ECUMENICAL PERSPECTIVE at 79, 93 (Thomas A. Howard ed., 2013).

6. John Tasioulas, Ch. 16, *Human Dignity and The Foundation of Human Rights*, at 292 in UNDERSTANDING HUMAN DIGNITY [hereinafter UNDERSTANDING DIGNITY], (Christopher McCrudden ed., 2013).

7. *Id. See* Jerry L. Mashaw, *Administrative Due Process: The Question of a Dignitary Theory*, 61 BOSTON U. L. REV. 885, 910–17 *passim* (1981).

8. BERNSTEIN, *supra* note 3 at 211.

9. *Id.* at 211.

10. *Id.* at 311.

11. William J. Brennan, *The Constitution of the United States: Contemporary Ratification*, 27 SO. TEX. L. REV. 433, 443 (1986).

12. *See* e.g., Aharon Barak, Ch. 20, *Human Dignity: The Constitutional Value and The Constitutional Rights*, at 380 in UNDERSTANDING DIGNITY, *supra* note 6. When interpreting the various rights enumerated in the Bill of Rights, dignity is, indeed, a significant interpretive value. AHARON BARAK, HUMAN DIGNITY: THE CONSTITUTIONAL VALUE AND THE CONSTITUTIONAL RIGHT 198–99, 206–08 (2015).

13. Michael Rosen, Ch. 7, *Dignity: The Case Against*, at 154 in UNDERSTANDING DIGNITY, *supra* note 6.

14. Weisstub, *supra* note 5.

15. *Id.*

16. Chaskalson, *supra* note 2 at 133. Central to the modern discourse of the history of human rights is the notion of dignity. For some, this principle is the closet to an internationally accepted framework for the normative regulation of political life that can be found. MICHAEL ROSEN, DIGNITY: ITS HISTORY AND MEANING, at 1 (2012). *See generally* ALASTAIR MacINTYRE, AFTER VIRTUE: A STUDY OF MORAL THEORY, Chs. 10–16 (3rd ed., 2007).

17. Weisstub, *supra* note 5 at 264.

18. Edmund Pellegrino, *Letter of Transmittal to the President of the United States* at xi, xii, and Ch. 20, *The Lived Experience of Human Dignity* at 513 in PRESIDENT'S COUNCIL ON BIOETHICS, HUMAN DIGNITY AND BIOETHICS: ESSAYS COMMISSIONED BY THE PRESIDENT'S COUNCIL ON BIOETHICS (2008).

19. Belinda J. Bennett, *Globalization in Health Rights in a Shrinking World* in BRAVE NEW WORLD OF HEALTH at 20 (Belinda J. Bennet et al. eds., 2008). The notion of a common morality is seen as compromising those norms that all morally serious persons accept as authoritative. THOMAS L. BEAUCHAMP & JAMES F. CHILDRESS, PRINCIPLES OF BIOMEDICAL ETHICS at 3 (5th ed., 2001). *See* KENNETH VEITCH, THE JURISDICTION OF MEDICAL LAW 23 (2007).

20. Weistubb, *supra* note 5. Another position sees dignity as a heuristic or "cognitive device" to aid in and resolving human rights issues. Rex D. Glensy, *The Right to Dignity*, 43 COLUM. HUM. RTS. L. REV. 65, 123 (2011).

21. *See* Ch. 7, *Advancing Global Frameworks for Decision Making, supra. See generally* George P. Smith, II, *Dignity in Living and in Dying*, 25 INDIANA J. GLOBAL LEGAL STUDIES 413 (2018).

22. Edmund D. Pellegrino, Ch. 20, *The Lived Experience of Human Dignity*, at 532 in HUMAN DIGNITY AND BIOETHICS, *supra* note 18.

23. *Id. See* Edmund D. Pellegrino, *Patient-Physician Autonomy: Conflicting Rights and Obligations in the Physician-Patient Relationship*, 10 J. CONTEMP. HEALTH L. & POL'Y 47 (1994). *See also* EDMUND D. PELLEGRINO & DAVID C. THOMASMA, FOR THE PATIENT'S OWN GOOD: THE RESTORATION OF BENEFICENCE IN HEALTH CARE (1988) at 27–27, 320–35 (explaining that beneficence acts to promote the best interests of the patient). *See generally* AI-JEN POO, THE AGE OF DIGNITY: PREPARING FOR THE ELDER BOOM IN A CHANGING AMERICA (2015) (suggesting how dignity in old age through home care can be achieved rather than placement in nursing homes); GEORGE P. SMITH, II, LAW AND BIOETHCS: INTERSECTIONS ALONG THE MORTAL COIL, Chs. 7, 8 (2012).

24. Amanda C. Pustilnik, *Pain As Fact and Heuristic: How Pain Neuroimaging Illuminates Moral Dimensions of Law* 97 CORNELL L. REV. 801, 825 n. 93 (2012). *See* ROB BODDICE, PAIN, Chs. 1, 7, 8 (2017).

25. George P. Smith, II, *Gently Into the Good Night: Toward a Compassionate Response to End-Stage Illness*, 22 TEMPLE POLITICAL & CIVIL RIGHTS L. REV. 475 (2013).

26. *See* Benjamin Zipursky, *De Shaney and the Jurisprudence of Compassion*, 65 N.Y.U. L. REV. 101 (1990).

27. *Id.*

28. *See* Lynne N. Henderson, *Legality and Empathy*, 85 MICH. L. REV. 1574, 1576 (1987).

29. Smith, *supra* note 25 at 481.

30. FIONA RANDALL & R. S. DOWNIE, PALLATIVE CARE ETHICS: A GOOD COMPANION 13 (1996).

31. *Id.* at 71. *See generally* VICTOR BROMBERT, MUSINGS ON MORTALITY (2013).

32. *See* George P. Smith, II, *Applying Bioethics in the 21st Century: Principlism or Situationism?* 30 J. CONTEMP. HEALTH L. & POL'Y 37 (2014). *See* L. W. SUMNER, PHYSICIAN-ASSISTED DEATH: WHAT EVERYONE NEEDS TO KNOW, Ch. 3 (2017). *See also* HARRY G. FRANKFURT, THE REASON OF LOVE (2004) (discussing how love is the most authoritative form of caring); Michael D. Kirby, *The New Biology and International Sharing—Lessons from the Life and Works of George Patrick Smith, II*, 7 INDIANA J. GLOBAL LEGAL STUDIES 425, 432–33 (2000) (discussing the force of human love and compassion as central to humane end-stage care).

33. *See* Amir Halevy, *Medical Futility, Patient Autonomy, and Professional Integrity: Finding the Appropriate Balance*, 18 HEALTH MATRIX 261, 286 (2008); Joseph J. Fins & Robert N. Swidler, *A Proposal to Restore Medical Futility as a Clinical Basis for DNR Order Under New York Law*, 22 NYSBA 37 (Spring, 2017). *See also* DAVID NAGEL, NEEDLESS SUFFERING: HOW SOCIETY FAILS THOSE WITH CHRONIC PAIN (2016); L. W. SUMNER, *id.*, at 100-03; LOIS SHEPHERD, IF THAT EVER HAPPENS TO ME (2009).

34. *See* GEORGE P. SMITH, II, PALLIATIVE CARE AND END-OF-LIFE DECISIONS (2013). *See generally* LEON KASS, LIFE, LIBERTY AND THE DEFENSE OF DIGNITY 247 (2002). During an illness, values are changing constantly. "You try to figure out what matters to you, and then you keep figuring it out." PAUL KALANITHI, WHEN BREATH BECOMES AIR 193 (2016).

35. FIONA RANDALL & ROBIN DOWNIE, END OF LIFE CHOICES: CONSENSUS AND CONTROVERSY 178 (2010). *See* GEORGE P. SMITH, II, BIOETHICS AND THE LAW: MEDICAL SOCIO LEGAL AND PHILOSOPHICAL DIRECTIONS FOR A BRAVE NEW WORLD, Ch. 11 (1993).

36. *See* Immaculada de Melo-Martes, *Human Dignity in International Policy Documents: A Useful Criteria for Public Policy?* 25 BIOETHICS 37 (2011); THERESE MURPHY, HEALTH AND HUMAN RIGHTS 41–42 (2013). *See generally* THE GLOBALIZATION OF HEALTH CARE: LEGAL AND ETHICAL ISSUES (I. Glenn Cohen ed., 2013).

37. *See generally* GEORGE P. SMITH, II, HUMAN RIGHTS AND BIOMEDICINE (2000). *See also* Appendix F, *infra*. Former United Nations Ambassador Bill Richards has observed that before America seeks to promote human dignity worldwide, it must first re-establish itself as a Nation "that honors human dignity." Bill Richards, *A New Human Rights Agenda for the U.S.: New Realism, Human Rights and The Rule of Law*, 21 HARV. HUMAN RIGHTS J. 1, 2 (2008). It strains the limits of credulity to accept the fact that while "the United States has played such a decisive role in shaping contemporary world order," it fails the test of leadership in the area of international human rights. HENRY KISSINGER, WORLD ORDER 234 (2014). *See* LOUIS HENKIN, THE RIGHTS OF MAN TODAY 116 (1978) (where the author terms the U.S. commitment to international human rights "less than wholehearted" and undistinguished).

38. Jordan J. Paust, *Human Dignity as a Constitutional Right: A Jurisprudentially Based Inquiry into Criteria and Content*, 72 HOWARD L. J. 145, 151 (1984). *See* GEORGE P. SMITH, II, *supra* note 23 at Ch. 4.

39. Glensy, *supra* note 20 at 142.

40. Klaus Dicke, *The Founding Function of Human Dignity in the Universal Declaration of Human Rights*, in CONCEPT OF HUMAN DIGNITY, *supra* note 1 at 111. *See* MARK P. LAGON & ANTHONY CLARK AREND, HUMAN DIGNITY AND THE FUTURE OF GLOBAL INSTITUTIONS (2014). *See also* Paolo G. Carozza, *The Universal Common Good and The Authority of International Law*, 9 LOGOS 28 (2006).

41. ELIZABETH WICKS, HUMAN RIGHTS AND HEALTHCARE 273 (2007).

42. WALTER KÄLIN & JORG KÜNZLI, THE LAW OF INTERNATIONAL HUMAN RIGHTS PROTECTION 303 (2004). Indeed, the same "minimal conditions necessary for a life of dignity" (e.g., autonomy, respect, compassion, humanness, decency, well-being) are the very same conditions that are in play in managing death. *See* Thaddeus M. Pope, *Legal History of Medical Aid in Dying: Physician Assisted Death in U.S. Courts and Legislatures*, 48 N. MEX. L. REV. 267 (2018). *See also* Smith, *supra* note 21.

43. Pellegrino, transmittal letter, *supra* note 18 at xii. *See* MYRES S. McDOUGAL, HAROLD D. LASSWELL, & LUNG-CHU CHEN, HUMAN RIGHTS AND WORLD PUBLIC ORDER 440 (1980) (acknowledging that in order to move forward "an optimum public order of human dignity," the peoples of the world need "perspectives" necessary to achieve this order). *See also* LEON KASS, *supra* note 34 at 246, concluding that, in the final analysis, dying with dignity "requires a dignity of soul in the human being who faces it." While acknowledging "the possibility of a humanly dignified facing of death can be destroyed or undermined from without . . . the actualization of that possibility depends largely on the soul, the character, the bearing of the dying man himself—that is, on things within." *Id.*

44. George P. Smith, II, *Social Justice and Health Care Management: An Elusive Quest?* 9 HOUS. J. HEALTH L. & POL'Y 1, 10 *passim* (2008).

45. Mary Ellen Caldwell, *Well-Being: Its Place Among Human Rights*, Ch. 6 at 196–97, in TOWARD WORLD ORDER AND HUMAN DIGNITY: ESSAYS IN HONOR OF MYRES S. McDOUGAL (W. Michael Reisman & Burns H. Westin eds., 1976). *See generally* Andrea Sangiovanni, HUMANITY WITHOUT DIGNITY: MORAL EQUALITY, RESPECT, AND HUMAN RIGHTS (2017); Michael D. Kirby, *Human Rights—The Challenge of The New Technology* 60 AUSTRALIAN L. J. 170 (1986).

Appendix A

The Charter of The United Nations

We The Peoples Of The United Nations
Determined

to save succeeding generations from the scourge of war, which twice in our life-time has brought untold sorrow to mankind, and
to reaffirm faith in fundamental human rights, in the dignity and worth of the human person, in the equal rights of men and women and of nations large and small, and
to establish conditions under which justice and respect for the obligations arising from treaties and other sources of international law can be maintained, and to promote social progress and better standards of life in larger freedom,

And For These Ends

to practice tolerance and live together in peace with one another as good neighbors, and
to unite our strength to maintain international peace and security, and
to ensure, by the acceptance of principles and the institution of methods, that armed force shall not be used, save in the common interest, and
to employ international machinery for the promotion of the economic and social advancement of all peoples,

Have Resolved To Combine Our Efforts
To Accomplish These Aims.[1]

Accordingly, our respective Governments, through representatives assembled in the city of San Francisco, who have exhibited their full powers found to be in good and due form, have agreed to the present Charter of the United Nations and do hereby establish an international organization to be known as the United Nations.

CHAPTER I
PURPOSES AND PRINCIPLES

Article 1

The Purposes of the United Nations are:

1. To maintain international peace and security, and to that end: to take effective collective measures for the prevention and removal of threats to the peace, and for the suppression of acts of aggression or other breaches of the peace, and to bring about by peaceful means, and in conformity with the principles of justice and international law, adjustment or settlement of international disputes or situations which might lead to a breach of the peace;
2. To develop friendly relations among nations based on respect for the principle of equal rights and self-determination of peoples, and to take other appropriate measures to strengthen universal peace;
3. To achieve international cooperation in solving international problems of an economic, social, cultural, or humanitarian character, and in promoting and encouraging respect for human rights and for fundamental freedoms for all without distinction as to race, sex, language, or religion; and
4. To be a center for harmonizing the actions of nations in the attainment of these common ends.

Article 2

The Organization and its Members, in pursuit of the Purposes stated in Article 1, shall act in accordance with the following Principles.

1. The Organization is based on the principle of the sovereign equality of all its Members.

2. All Members, in order to ensure to all of them the rights and benefits resulting from membership, shall fulfil in good faith the obligations assumed by them in accordance with the present Charter.
3. All Members shall settle their international disputes by peaceful means in such a manner that international peace and security, and justice, are not endangered.
4. All Members shall refrain in their international relations from the threat or use of force against the territorial integrity or political independence of any state, or in any other manner inconsistent with the Purposes of the United Nations.
5. All Members shall give the United Nations every assistance in any action it takes in accordance with the present Charter, and shall refrain from giving assistance to any state against which the United Nations is taking preventive or enforcement action.
6. The Organization shall ensure that states which are not Members of the United Nations act in accordance with these Principles so far as may be necessary for the maintenance of international peace and security.
7. Nothing contained in the present Charter shall authorize the United Nations to intervene in matters which are essentially within the domestic jurisdiction of any state or shall require the Members to submit such matters to settlement under the present Charter; but this principle shall not prejudice the application of enforcement measures under Chapter VII.

. . . .

CHAPTER IX
INTERNATIONAL ECONOMIC AND SOCIAL COOPERATION

Article 55

With a view to the creation of conditions of stability and well-being which are necessary for peaceful and friendly relations among nations based on respect for the principle of equal rights and self-determination of peoples, the United Nations shall promote:

a. higher standards of living, full employment, and conditions of economic and social progress and development;
b. solutions of international economic, social, health, and related problems; and international cultural and educational cooperation; and

c. universal respect for, and observance of, human rights and fundamental freedoms for all without distinction as to race, sex, language, or religion.

Article 56

All Members pledge themselves to take joint and separate action in cooperation with the Organization for the achievement of the purposes set forth in Article 55.

Article 57

1. The various specialized agencies, established by intergovernmental agreement and having wide international responsibilities, as defined in their basic instruments, in economic, social, cultural, educational, health, and related fields, shall be brought into relationship with the United Nations in accordance with the provisions of Article 63.
2. Such agencies thus brought into relationship with the United Nations are hereinafter referred to as specialized agencies.

Article 58

The Organization shall make recommendations for the coordination of the policies and activities of the specialized agencies.

Article 59

The Organization shall, where appropriate, initiate negotiations among the states concerned for the creation of any new specialized agencies required for the accomplishment of the purposes set forth in Article 55.

Article 60

Responsibility for the discharge of the functions of the Organization set forth in this Chapter shall be vested in the General Assembly, in the Economic and Social Council, which shall have for this purpose the powers set forth in Chapter X.

. . . .

CHAPTER XI
DECLARATION REGARDING NON-SELF-GOVERNING TERRITORIES

Article 73

Members of the United Nations which have or assume responsibilities for the administration of territories whose peoples have not yet attained a full measure of self-government recognize the principle that the interests of the inhabitants of these territories are paramount, and accept as a sacred trust the obligation to promote to the utmost, within the system of international peace and security established by the present Charter, the well-being of the inhabitants of these territories, and, to this end:

a. to ensure, with due respect for the culture of the peoples concerned, their political, economic, social, and educational advancement, their just treatment, and their protection against abuses;
b. to develop self-government, to take due account of the political aspirations of the peoples, and to assist them in the progressive development of their free political institutions, according to the particular circumstances of each territory and its peoples and their varying stages of advancement;
c. to further international peace and security;
d. to promote constructive measures of development, to encourage research, and to cooperate with one another and, when and where appropriate, with specialized international bodies with a view to the practical achievement of the social, economic, and scientific purposes set forth in this Article; and
e. to transmit regularly to the Secretary-General for information purposes, subject to such limitation as security and constitutional considerations may require, statistical and other information of a technical nature relating to economic, social, and educational conditions in the territories for which they are respectively responsible other than those territories to which Chapters XII and XIII apply.

Article 74

Members of the United Nations also agree that their policy in respect of the territories to which this Chapter applies, no less than in respect of their metropolitan areas, must be based on the general principle of good-neighborliness, due account being taken of the interests and well-being of the rest of the world, in social, economic, and commercial matters.

NOTE

1. The Charter of The United Nations, Oct. 24, 1945, 1 U.N.T.S. XVI.

Appendix B

The Universal Declaration of Human Rights

PREAMBLE

Whereas recognition of the inherent dignity and of the equal and inalienable rights of all members of the human family is the foundation of freedom, justice and peace in the world,

Whereas disregard and contempt for human rights have resulted in barbarous acts which have outraged the conscience of mankind, and the advent of a world in which human beings shall enjoy freedom of speech and belief and freedom from fear and want has been proclaimed as the highest aspiration of the common people,

Whereas it is essential, if man is not to be compelled to have recourse, as a last resort, to rebellion against tyranny and oppression, that human rights should be protected by the rule of law,

Whereas it is essential to promote the development of friendly relations between nations,

Whereas the peoples of the United Nations have in the Charter reaffirmed their faith in fundamental human rights, in the dignity and worth of the human person and in the equal rights of men and women and have determined to promote social progress and better standards of life in larger freedom,

Whereas Member States have pledged themselves to achieve, in cooperation with the United Nations, the promotion of universal respect for and observance of human rights and fundamental freedoms,

Whereas a common understanding of these rights and freedoms is of the greatest importance for the full realization of this pledge,

Now, therefore,

The General Assembly,

Proclaims this Universal Declaration of Human Rights as a common standard of achievement for all peoples and all nations, to the end that every individual and every organ of society, keeping this Declaration constantly in mind, shall strive by teaching and education to promote respect for these rights and freedoms and by progressive measures, national and international, to secure their universal and effective recognition and observance, both among the peoples of Member States themselves and among the peoples of territories under their jurisdiction.[1]

ARTICLE 1

All human beings are born free and equal in dignity and rights. They are endowed with reason and conscience and should act towards one another in a spirit of brotherhood.

ARTICLE 2

Everyone is entitled to all the rights and freedoms set forth in this Declaration, without distinction of any kind, such as race, colour, sex, language, religion, political or other opinion, national or social origin, property, birth or other status. Furthermore, no distinction shall be made on the basis of the political, jurisdictional or international status of the country or territory to which a person belongs, whether it be independent, trust, non-self-governing or under any other limitation of sovereignty.

ARTICLE 3

Everyone has the right to life, liberty and security of person.

ARTICLE 4

No one shall be held in slavery or servitude; slavery and the slave trade shall be prohibited in all their forms.

ARTICLE 5

No one shall be subjected to torture or to cruel, inhuman or degrading treatment or punishment.

ARTICLE 6

Everyone has the right to recognition everywhere as a person before the law.

ARTICLE 7

All are equal before the law and are entitled without any discrimination to equal protection of the law. All are entitled to equal protection against any discrimination in violation of this Declaration and against any incitement to such discrimination.

ARTICLE 8

Everyone has the right to an effective remedy by the competent national tribunals for acts violating the fundamental rights granted him by the constitution or by law.

ARTICLE 9

No one shall be subjected to arbitrary arrest, detention or exile.

ARTICLE 10

Everyone is entitled in full equality to a fair and public hearing by an independent and impartial tribunal, in the determination of his rights and obligations and of any criminal charge against him.

ARTICLE 11

1. Everyone charged with a penal offence has the right to be presumed innocent until proved guilty according to law in a public trial at which he has had all the guarantees necessary for his defense.
2. No one shall be held guilty of any penal offence on account of any act or omission which did not constitute a penal offence, under national or international law, at the time when it was committed. Nor shall a heavier penalty be imposed than the one that was applicable at the time the penal offence was committed.

ARTICLE 12

No one shall be subjected to arbitrary interference with his privacy, family, home or correspondence, nor to attacks upon his honour and reputation. Everyone has the right to the protection of the law against such interference or attacks.

ARTICLE 13

1. Everyone has the right to freedom of movement and residence within the borders of each State.
2. Everyone has the right to leave any country, including his own, and to return to his country.

ARTICLE 14

1. Everyone has the right to seek and to enjoy in other countries asylum from persecution.
2. This right may not be invoked in the case of prosecutions genuinely arising from non-political crimes or from acts contrary to the purposes and principles of the United Nations.

ARTICLE 15

1. Everyone has the right to a nationality.
2. No one shall be arbitrarily deprived of his nationality nor denied the right to change his nationality.

ARTICLE 16

1. Men or women of full age, without any limitation due to race, nationality or religion, have the right to marry and to found a family. They are entitled to equal rights as to marriage, during marriage and at its dissolution.
2. Marriage shall be entered into only with the free and full consent of the intending spouses.
3. The family is the natural and fundamental group unit of society and is entitled to protection by society and the State.

ARTICLE 17

1. Everyone has the right to own property alone as well as in association with others.
2. No one shall be arbitrarily deprived of his property.

ARTICLE 18

Everyone has the right to freedom of thought, conscience and religion; this right includes freedom to change his religion or belief, and freedom, either alone or in community with others and in public or private, to manifest his religion or belief in teaching, practice, worship and observance.

ARTICLE 19

Everyone has the right to freedom of opinion and expression; this right includes freedom to hold opinions without interference and to seek, receive and impart information and ideas through any media and regardless of frontiers.

ARTICLE 20

1. Everyone has the right to freedom of peaceful assembly and association.
2. No one may be compelled to belong to an association.

ARTICLE 21

1. Everyone has the right to take part in the government of his country, directly or through freely chosen representatives.
2. Everyone has the right to equal access to public service in his country.
3. The will of the people shall be the basis of the authority of government; this will shall be expressed in periodic and genuine elections which shall be by universal and equal suffrage and shall be held by secret vote or by equivalent free voting procedures.

ARTICLE 22

Everyone, as a member of society, has the right to social security and is entitled to realization, through national effort and international co-operation and in accordance with the organization and resources of each State, of the economic, social and cultural rights indispensable for his dignity and the free development of his personality.

ARTICLE 23

1. Everyone has the right to work, to free choice of employment, to just and favourable conditions of work and to protection against unemployment.
2. Everyone, without any discrimination, has the right to equal pay for equal work.
3. Everyone who works has the right to just and favourable remuneration ensuring for himself and his family an existence worthy of human dignity, and supplemented, if necessary, by other means of social protection.

4. Everyone has the right to form and to join trade unions for the protection of his interests.

ARTICLE 24

Everyone has the right to rest and leisure, including reasonable limitation of working hours and periodic holidays with pay.

ARTICLE 25

1. Everyone has the right to a standard of living adequate for the health and well-being of himself and of his family, including food, clothing, housing and medical care and necessary social services, and the right to security in the event of unemployment, sickness, disability, widowhood, old age or other lack of livelihood in circumstances beyond his control.
2. Motherhood and childhood are entitled to special care and assistance. All children, whether born in or out of wedlock, shall enjoy the same social protection.

ARTICLE 26

1. Everyone has the right to education. Education shall be free, at least in the elementary and fundamental stages. Elementary education shall be compulsory. Technical and professional education shall be made generally available and higher education shall be equally accessible to all on the basis of merit.
2. Education shall be directed to the full development of the human personality and to the strengthening of respect for human rights and fundamental freedoms. It shall promote understanding, tolerance and friendship among all nations, racial or religious groups, and shall further the activities of the United Nations for the maintenance of peace.
3. Parents have a prior right to choose the kind of education that shall be given to their children.

ARTICLE 27

1. Everyone has the right freely to participate in the cultural life of the community, to enjoy the arts and to share in scientific advancement and its benefits.
2. Everyone has the right to the protection of the moral and material interests resulting from any scientific, literary or artistic production of which he is the author.

ARTICLE 28

Everyone is entitled to a social and international order in which the rights and freedoms set forth in this Declaration can be fully realized.

ARTICLE 29

1. Everyone has duties to the community in which alone the free and full development of his personality is possible.
2. In the exercise of his rights and freedoms, everyone shall be subject only to such limitations as are determined by law solely for the purpose of securing due recognition and respect for the rights and freedoms of others and of meeting the just requirements of morality, public order and the general welfare in a democratic society.
3. These rights and freedoms may in no case be exercised contrary to the purposes and principles of the United Nations.

ARTICLE 30

Nothing in this Declaration may be interpreted as implying for any State, group or person any right to engage in any activity or to perform any act aimed at the destruction of any of the rights and freedoms set forth herein.

NOTES

1. Universal Declaration of Human Rights, G. A. Res. 217 A (III), U.N. Doc. A/810 at 7 (1948).

Appendix C

The United Nations International Covenant on Economic, Social, and Cultural Rights

PREAMBLE

The States Parties to the present Covenant
Considering that, in accordance with the principles proclaimed in the Charter of the United Nations, recognition of the inherent dignity and of the equal and inalienable rights of all the members of the human family is the foundation of freedom, justice and peace in world,

Recognizing that these rights derive from the inherent dignity of the human person.

Recognizing that, in accordance with the Universal Declaration of Human Rights, the ideal of free human beings enjoying freedom from fear and want can only be achieved if conditions are created whereby everyone may enjoy his economic, social and cultural rights, as well as his civil and political rights and freedom,

Realizing that the individual, having duties to other individuals and to the community to which he belongs, is under a responsibility to strive for the promotion and observance of the rights recognized in the present Covenant,

Agree upon the following articles:

PART I

Article 1

1. All peoples have the right of self-determination.[1] By virtue of that right they freely determine their political status and freely pursue their economic, social and cultural development.
2. All peoples may, for their own ends, freely dispose of their natural wealth and resources without prejudice to any obligations arising out of international economic co-operation, based upon the principle of mutual benefit, and international law. In no case may a people be deprived of its own means of subsistence.
3. The States Parties to the present Covenant, including those having responsibility for the administration of Non-Self-Governing and Trust Territories, shall promote the realization of the right of self-determination, and shall respect that right, in conformity with the provisions of the Charter of the United Nations.

PART II

Article 2

1. Each State Party to the present Covenant undertakes to take steps, individually and through international assistance and co-operation, especially economic and technical, to the maximum of its available resources, with a view to achieving progressively the full realization of the rights recognized in the present Covenant by all appropriate means, including particularly the adoption of legislative measures.
2. The States Parties to present Covenant undertake to guarantee that the rights enunciated in the present Covenant will be exercised without discrimination of any kind as to race, colour, sex, language, religion, political or other opinion, national or social origin, property, birth or other status.
3. Developing countries, with due regard to human rights and their national economy, may determine to what extent they would guarantee the economic rights recognized in the present Covenant to non-nationals.

Article 3

The States Parties to the present Covenant undertake to ensure the equal right of men and women to the enjoyment of all economic, social and cultural rights set forth in the present Covenant.

Article 4

The States Parties to the present Covenant recognize that, in the enjoyment of those rights provided by the State in conformity with the present Covenant, the State may subject such rights only to such limitations as are determined by law only in so far as this may be compatible with the nature of these rights and solely for the purpose of promoting the general welfare in a democratic society.

Article 5

1. Nothing in the present Covenant may be interpreted as implying for any State, group or person any right to engage in any activity or to perform any act aimed at the destruction of any of the rights or freedoms recognized herein, or at their limitation to greater extent than is provided for in the present Covenant.
2. No restriction upon or derogation from any of the fundamental human rights recognized or existing in any country in virtue of law, conventions, regulations or custom shall be admitted on the pretext that the present Covenant does not recognize such rights or that it recognizes them to a lesser extent.

PART III

Article 6

1. The States Parties to the present Covenant recognize the right to work, which includes the right of everyone to the opportunity to gain his living by work which he freely chooses or accepts, and will take appropriate steps to safeguard this right.
2. The Steps to be taken by a State Party to the present Covenant to achieve the full realization of this right shall include technical and vocational guidance and training programmes, policies and techniques to achieve steady economic, social and cultural development and full and productive

employment under conditions safeguarding fundamental political and economic freedoms to the individual.

Article 7

The States to the present Covenant recognize the right of everyone to the enjoyment of just and favourable conditions of work, which ensure, in particular:

1. Remuneration which provides all workers, as a minimum, with:
    1. Fair wages and equal remuneration for work of equal value without distinction of any kind, in particular women being guaranteed conditions of work not inferior to those enjoyed by men, with equal pay for equal work;
    2. A decent living for themselves and their families in accordance with the provisions of the present Covenant;
2. Safe and healthy working conditions;
3. Equal opportunity for everyone to be promoted in his employment to an appropriate higher level, subject to no considerations other than those of seniority and competence;
4. Rest, leisure and reasonable limitation of working hours and periodic holidays with pay, as well as remuneration for public holidays.

. . . .

Article 9

The States Parties to the present Covenant recognize the right of everyone to social security, including social insurance.

Article 10

The States Parties to the present Covenant recognize that:

1. The widest possible protection and assistance should be accorded to the family, which is the natural and fundamental group unit of society, particularly for its establishment and while it is responsible for the care and education of dependent children. Marriage must be entered into with the free consent of the intending spouses.
2. Special protection should be accorded to mothers during a reasonable period before and after childbirth. During such period working mothers

should be accorded paid leave or leave with adequate social security benefits.

3. Special measures of protection and assistance should be taken on behalf of all children and young persons without any discrimination for reasons of parentage or other conditions. Children and young persons should be protected from economic and social exploitation. Their employment in work harmful to their morals or health or dangerous to life or likely to hamper their normal development should be punishable by law. States should also set age limits below which the paid employment of child labour should be prohibited and punishable by law.

Article 11

1. The States Parties to present Covenant recognize the right of everyone to an adequate standard of living for himself and his family, including adequate food, clothing and housing, and to the continuous improvement of living conditions. The States Parties will take appropriate steps to ensure the international co-operation based on free consent.
2. The States Parties to present Covenant, recognizing the fundamental right of everyone to be free from hunger, shall take, individually and through international co-operation, the measures, including specific programmes, which are needed:
    1. To improve methods of production, conservation and distribution of food by making full use of technical and scientific knowledge, by disseminating knowledge of the principles of nutrition and by developing or reforming agrarian systems in such a way as to achieve the most efficient development and utilization of natural resources;
    2. Taking into account the problems of both food-importing and food-exporting countries, to ensure an equitable distribution of world food supplies in relation to need.

Article 12

1. The States Parties to the present Covenant recognize the right of everyone to the enjoyment of the highest attainable standard of physical and mental health.
2. The steps to be taken by the States Parties to the present Covenant to achieve the full realization of this right shall include those necessary for:
    1. The provision for the reduction of the stillbirth-rate and of infant mortality and for the healthy development of the child;

2. The improvement of all aspects of environmental and industrial hygiene;
3. The prevention, treatment and control epidemic, endemic, occupational and other diseases;
4. The creation of conditions which would assure to all medical service and medical attention in the event of sickness.

Article 13

1. The States Parties to the present Covenant recognize the right of everyone to education. They agree that education shall be directed to the full development of the human personality and the sense of its dignity, and shall strengthen the respect for human rights and fundamental freedoms. They further agree that education shall enable all persons to participate effectively in a free society, promote understanding, tolerance and friendship among all nations and all racial, ethnic or religious groups, and further the activities of the United Nations for the maintenance of peace.
2. The States Parties to the present Covenant recognize that, with a view to achieving the full realization of this right:
    1. Primary education shall be compulsory and available free to all;
    2. Secondary education in its different forms, including technical and vocational secondary education, shall be made generally available and accessible to all by ever appropriate means, and in particular by the progressive introduction of free education;
    3. Higher education shall be made equally accessible to all, on the basis of capacity, by every appropriate means, and in particular by the progressive introduction of free education;
    4. Fundamental education shall be encouraged or intensified as far as possible for those persons who have not received or completed the whole period of their primary education;
    5. The development of a system of schools at all levels shall be actively pursued, an adequate fellowship system shall be established, and the material conditions of teaching staff shall be continuously improved.
3. The States Parties to the present Covenant undertake to have respect for the liberty of parents and, when applicable, legal guardians to choose for their children schools, other than those established by the public authorities, which conform to such minimum educational standards as may be laid down or approved by the State and to ensure the religious and moral education of their children in conformity with their own convictions.
4. No part of this article shall be construed so as to interfere with the liberty of individuals and bodies to establish and direct educational institutions, subject always to the observance of the principles set forth in paragraph

1 or this article and to the requirement that the education given in such institutions shall conform to such minimum standards as may be laid down by the State.

Article 14

Each state Party to the present Covenant which, at the time of becoming a Party, has not been able to secure in its metropolitan territory of other territories under its jurisdiction compulsory primary education, free of charge, undertakes, within two years, to work out and adopt a detailed plan of action for the progressive implementation, within a reasonable number of years, to be fixed in the plan, of the principle of compulsory education free of charge for all.

Article 15

1. The States Parties to the present covenant recognize the right of everyone:
   1. To take part in cultural life;
   2. To enjoy the benefits of scientific progress and its applications;
   3. To benefit from the protection of the moral and material interests resulting from any scientific, literary or artistic production of which he is the author.
2. The steps to be taken by the States Parties to the present Covenant to achieve the full realization of this right shall include those necessary for the conservation, the development and the diffusion of science and culture.
3. The States Parties to the present Covenant undertake to respect the freedom indispensable for scientific research and creative activity.
4. The States Parties to the present Covenant recognize the benefits to be derived from the encouragement and development of international contacts and co-operation in the scientific and cultural fields.

PART IV

Article 16

1. The States Parties to the present Covenant undertake to submit in conformity with this part of the Covenant reports on the measures which they have adopted and the progress made in achieving the observance of the rights recognized herein.

2.
 (a) All reports shall be submitted to Secretary-General of the United Nations, who shall transmit copies to the Economic and Social Council for consideration in accordance with the provisions of the present Covenant;
 (b) The Secretary-General of the United Nations shall also transmit to the specialized agencies copies of the reports, or any relevant parts therefrom, from States Parties to the present Covenant which are also members of these specialized agencies in so far as these reports, or parts therefrom, relate to any matters which fall within the responsibilities of the said agencies in accordance with their constitutional instruments.

Article 17

1. The States Parties to the present Covenant shall furnish their reports in stages, in accordance with a programme to be established by the Economic and Social Council within one year of the entry into force of the present Covenant after consultation with the States Parties and the specialized agencies concerned.
2. Reports may indicate factors and difficulties affecting the degree of fulfillment of obligations under the present Covenant.
3. Where relevant information has previously been furnished to the United Nations or to any specialized agency by any State Party to the present Covenant, it will not be necessary to reproduce that information, but a precise reference to the information so furnished will suffice.

Article 18

Pursuant to its responsibilities under the Charter of the United Nations in the field of human rights and fundamental freedoms, the Economic and Social Council may make arrangements with the specialized agencies in respect of their reporting to it on the progress made in achieving the observance of the provisions of the present Covenant falling within the scope of their activities. These reports may include particulars of decisions and recommendations on such implementation adopted by their competent organs.

Article 19

The Economic and Social Council may transmit to the Commission on Human Rights for study and general recommendation or, as appropriate, for information the reports concerning human rights submitted by States in accordance with articles 16 and 17, and those concerning human rights submitted by the specialized agencies in accordance with article 18.

. . . .

NOTE

1. The United Nations International Covenant On Economic, Social And Cultural Rights, 993 U.N.T.S. at 3 (1976).

Appendix D

The United Nations International Covenant on Civil and Political Rights

PREAMBLE

The States Parties to the present Covenant,

Considering that, in accordance with the principles proclaimed in the Charter of the United Nations, recognition of the inherent dignity and of the equal and inalienable rights of all members of the human family is the foundation of freedom, justice and peace in the world,

Recognizing that these rights derive from the inherent dignity of the human person,

Recognizing that, in accordance with the Universal Declaration of Human Rights, the ideal of free human beings enjoying civil and political freedom and freedom from fear and want can only be achieved if conditions are created whereby everyone may enjoy his civil and political rights, as well his economic, social and cultural rights,

Considering the obligation of States under the Charter of the United Nations to promote universal respect for, and observance of, human rights and freedoms,

Realizing that the individual, having duties to other individuals and to the community to which he belongs, is under a responsibility to strive for the promotion and observance of the rights recognized in the present Covenant,

Agree upon the following articles:

PART I

Article 1

1. All peoples have the right of self-determination.[1] By virtue of that right they freely determine their political status and freely pursue their economic, social and cultural development.
2. All peoples may, for their own ends, freely dispose of their natural wealth and resources without prejudice to any obligations arising out of international economic co-operation, based upon the principle of mutual benefit, and international law. In no case may a people be deprived of its own means of subsistence.
3. The States Parties to the present Covenant, including those having responsibility for the administration of Non-Self-Governing and Trust Territories, shall promote the realization of the right of self-determination, and shall respect that right, in conformity with the provisions of the Charter of the United Nations.

PART II

Article 2

1. Each State Party to the present Covenant undertakes to respect and to ensure to all individuals within its territory and subject to its jurisdiction the rights recognized in the present Covenant, without distinction of any kind, such as race, colour, sex, language, religion, political or other opinion, national or social origin, property, birth or other status.
2. Where not already provided for by existing legislative or other measures, each State Party to the present Covenant undertakes to take the necessary steps, in accordance with its constitutional processes and with the provisions of the present Covenant, to adopt such laws or other measures as may be necessary to give effect to the rights recognized in the present Covenant.
3. Each State Party to the present Covenant undertakes:
   (a) To ensure that any person whose rights or freedoms as herein recognized are violated shall have an effective remedy, notwithstanding

that the violation has been committed by persons acting in an official capacity;

(b) To ensure that any person claiming such a remedy shall have his right thereto determined by competent judicial, administrative or legislative authorities, or by any other competent authority provided for by the legal system of the State, and to develop the possibilities of judicial remedy;

(c) To ensure that the competent authorities shall enforce such remedies when granted.

Article 3

The States Parties to the present Covenant undertake to ensure the equal right of men and women to the enjoyment of all civil and political rights set forth in the present Covenant.

Article 4

1. In time of public emergency which threatens the life of the nation and the existence of which is officially proclaimed, the States Parties to the present Covenant may take measures derogating from their obligations under the present Covenant to the extent strictly required by the exigencies of the situation, provided that such measures are not inconsistent with their other obligations under international law and do not involve discrimination solely on the ground of race, colour, sex, languge, religion or social origin.
2. No derogation from articles 6, 7, 8 (paragraphs 1 and 2), 11, 15, 16 and 18 may be made under this provision.
3. Any State Party to the present Covenant availing itself of the right of derogation shall immediately inform the other States Parties to the present Covenant, through the intermediary of the Secretary-General of the United Nations, of the provisions from which it has derogated and of the reasons by which it was actuated. A further communication shall be made, through the same intermediary, on the date on which it terminates such derogation.

Article 5

1. Nothing in the present Covenant may be interpreted as implying for any State, group or person any right to engage in any activity or perform any act aimed at the destruction of any of the rights and freedoms recognized herein or at their limitation to a greater extent than is provided for in the present Covenant.

2. There shall be no restriction upon or derogation from any of the fundamental human rights recognized or existing in any State Party to the present Covenant pursuant to law, conventions, regulations or custom on the pretext that the present Covenant does not recognize such rights or that it recognizes them to a lesser extent.

PART III

Article 6

1. Every human being has the inherent right to life. This right shall be protected by law. No one shall be arbitrarily deprived of his life.
2. In countries which have not abolished the death penalty, sentence of death may be imposed only for the most serious crimes in accordance with the law in force at the time of the commission of the crime and not contrary to the provisions of the present Covenant and to the Convention on the Prevention and Punishment of the Crime of Genocide. This penalty can only be carried out pursuant to a final judgement rendered by a competent court.
3. When deprivation of life constitutes the crime of genocide, it is understood that nothing in this article shall authorize any State Party to the present Covenant to derogate in any way from any obligation assumed under the provisions of the Convention on the Prevention and Punishment of the Crime of Genocide.
4. Anyone sentenced to death shall have the right to seek pardon or commutation of the sentence. Amnesty, pardon or commutation of the sentence of death may be granted in all cases.
5. Sentence of death shall not be imposed for crimes committed by persons below eighteen years of age and shall not be carried out on pregnant women.
6. Nothing in this article shall be invoked to delay or to prevent the abolition of capital punishment by any State Party to the present Covenant.

Article 7

No one shall be subjected to torture or to cruel, inhuman or degrading treatment or punishment. In particular, no one shall be subjected without his free consent to medical or scientific experimentation.

ARTICLE 8

1. No one shall be held in slavery; slavery and the slave-trade in all their forms shall be prohibited.
2. No one shall be held in servitude.
3.
   (a) No one shall be required to perform forced or compulsory labour;
   (b) Paragraph 3 (a) shall not be held to preclude, in countries where imprisonment with hard labour may be imposed as a punishment for a crime, the performance of hard labour in pursuance of a sentence to such punishment by a competent court;
   (c) For the purpose of this paragraph the term "forced or compulsory labour" shall not include:
      (i) Any work or service, not referred to in subparagraph (b), normally required of a person who is under detention in consequence of a lawful order of a court, or of a person during conditional release from such detention;
      (ii) Any service of a military character and, in countries where conscientious objection is recognized, any national service required by law of conscientious objectors;
      (iii) Any service exacted in cases of emergency or calamity threatening the life or well-being of the community;
      (iv) Any work or service which forms part of normal civil obligations.

Article 9

1. Everyone has the right to liberty and security of person. No one shall be subjected to arbitrary arrest or detention. No one shall be deprived of his liberty except on such grounds and in accordance with such procedure as are established by law.
2. Anyone who is arrested shall be informed, at the time of arrest, of the reasons for his arrest and shall be promptly informed of any charges against him.
3. Anyone arrested or detained on a criminal charge shall be brought promptly before a judge or other officer authorized by law to exercise judicial power and shall be entitled to trial within a reasonable time or to release. It shall not be the general rule that persons awaiting trial shall be detained in custody, but release may be subject to guarantees to appear for trial, at any other stage of the judicial proceedings, and, should occasion arise, for execution of the judgement.

4. Anyone who is deprived of his liberty by arrest or detention shall be entitled to take proceedings before a court, in order that that court may decide without delay on the lawfulness of his detention and order his release if the detention is not lawful.
5. Anyone who has been the victim of unlawful arrest or detention shall have an enforceable right to compensation.

Article 10

1. All persons deprived of their liberty shall be treated with humanity and with respect for the inherent dignity of the human person.
2.
   (a) Accused persons shall, save in exceptional circumstances, be segregated from convicted persons and shall be subject to separate treatment appropriate to their status as unconvicted persons;
   (b) Accused juvenile persons shall be separated from adults and brought as speedily as possible for adjudication.
3. The penitentiary system shall comprise treatment of prisoners the essential aim of which shall be their reformation and social rehabilitation. Juvenile offenders shall be segregated from adults and be accorded treatment appropriate to their age and legal status.

Article 11

No one shall be imprisoned merely on the ground of inability to fulfil a contractual obligation.

Article 12

1. Everyone lawfully within the territory of a State shall, within that territory, have the right to liberty of movement and freedom to choose his residence.
2. Everyone shall be free to leave any country, including his own.
3. The above-mentioned rights shall not be subject to any restrictions except those which are provided by law, are necessary to protect national security, public order (ordre public), pubic health or morals or the rights and freedoms of others, and are consistent with the other rights recognized in the present Covenant.
4. No one shall be arbitrarily deprived of the right to enter his own country.

Article 13

An alien lawfully in the territory of a State Party to the present Covenant may be expelled therefrom only in pursuance of a decision reached in accordance with law and shall, except where compelling reasons of national security otherwise require, be allowed to submit the reasons against his expulsion and to have his case reviewed by, and be represented for the purpose before, the competent authority or a person or persons especially designated by the competent authority.

Article 14

1. All persons shall be equal before the courts and tribunals. In the determination of any criminal charge against him, or of his rights and obligations in a suit at law, everyone shall be entitled to a fair and public hearing by a competent, independent and impartial tribunal established by law. The press and the public may be excluded from all or part of a trial for reasons of morals, public order (ordre public) or national security in a democratic society, or when the interest of the private lives of the parties so requires, or to the extent strictly necessary in the opinion of the court in special circumstances where publicity would prejudice the interests of justice; but any judgement rendered in a criminal case or in a suit at law shall be made public except where the interest of juvenile persons otherwise requires or the proceedings concern matrimonial disputes or the guardianship of children.
2. Everyone charged with a criminal offence shall have the right to be presumed innocent until proved guilty according to law.
3. In the determination of any criminal charge against him, everyone shall be entitled to the following minimum guarantees, in full equality:
   (a) To be informed promptly and in detail in a language which he understands of the nature and cause of the charge against him;
   (b) To have adequate time and facilities for the preparation of his defense and to communicate with counsel of his own choosing;
   (c) To be tried without undue delay;
   (d) To be tried in his presence, and to defend himself in person or through legal assistance of his own choosing; to be informed, if he does not have legal assistance, of this right; and to have legal assistance assigned to him, in any case where the interests of justice so require, and without payment by him in any such case if he does not have sufficient means to pay for it;

(e) To examine, or have examined, the witnesses against him and to obtain the attendance and examination of witnesses on his behalf under the same conditions as witnesses against him;
(f) To have the free assistance of an interpreter if he cannot understand or speak the language used in court;
(g) Not to be compelled to testify against himself or to confess guilt.

4. In the case of juvenile persons, the procedure shall be such as will take account of their age and the desirability of promoting their rehabilitation.
5. Everyone convicted of a crime shall have the right to his conviction and sentence being reviewed by a higher tribunal according to law.
6. When a person has by a final decision been convicted of a criminal offence and when subsequently his conviction has been reversed or he has been pardoned on the ground that a new or newly discovered fact shows conclusively that there has been a miscarriage of justice, the person who has suffered punishment as a result of such conviction shall be compensated according to law, unless it is proved that the non-disclosure of the unknown fact in time is wholly or partly attributable to him.
7. No one shall be liable to be tried or punished again for an offence for which he has already been finally convicted or acquitted in accordance with the law and penal procedure of each country.

Article 15

1. No one shall be held guilty of any criminal offence on account of any act or omission which did not constitute a criminal offence, under national or international law, at the time when it was committed. Nor shall a heavier penalty be imposed than the one that was applicable at the timer when the criminal offence was committed. If, subsequent to the commission of the offence, provision is made by law for the imposition of the lighter penalty, the offender shall benefit thereby.
2. Nothing in this article shall prejudice the trial and punishment of any person for any act or omission which, at the time when it was committed, was criminal according to the general principles of law recognized by the community of nations.

Article 16

Everyone shall have the right to recognition everywhere as a person before the law.

Article 17

1. No one shall be subjected to arbitrary or unlawful interference with his privacy, family, home or correspondence, nor to unlawful attacks on his honour and reputation.
2. Everyone has the right to the protection of the law against such interference or attacks.

Article 18

1. Everyone shall have the right to freedom of thought, conscience and religion. This right shall include freedom to have or to adopt a religion or belief of his choice, and freedom, either individually or in community with others and in public or private, to manifest his religion or belief in worship, observance, practice and teaching.
2. No one shall be subject to coercion which would impair his freedom to have or to adopt a religion or belief of his choice.
3. Freedom to manifest one's religion or beliefs may be subject only to such limitations as are prescribed by law and are necessary to protect public safety, order, health, or morals or the fundamental rights and freedoms of others.
4. The States Parties to the present Covenant undertake to have respect for the liberty of parents and, when applicable, legal guardians to ensure the religious and moral education of their children in conformity with their own convictions.

Article 19

1. Everyone shall have the right to hold opinions without interference.
2. Everyone shall have the right to freedom of expression; this right shall include freedom to seek, receive and impart information and ideas of all kinds, regardless of frontiers, either orally, in writing or in print, in the form of art, or through any other media of his choice.
3. The exercise of the rights provided for in paragraph 2 of this article carries with it special duties and responsibilities. It may therefore be subject to certain restrictions, but these shall only be such as are provided by law and are necessary:
   (a) For respect of the rights or reputations of others;
   (b) For the protection of national security or of public order (ordre public), or of public health or morals.

Article 20

1. Any propaganda for war shall be prohibited by law.
2. Any advocacy of national, racial or religious hatred that constitutes incitement to discrimination, hostility or violence shall be prohibited by law.

Article 21

The right of peaceful assembly shall be recognized. No restrictions may be placed on the exercise of this right other than those imposed in conformity with the law and which are necessary in a democratic society in the interests of national security or public safety, public order (ordre public), the protection of public health or morals or the protection of the rights and freedoms of others.

Article 22

1. Everyone shall have the right to freedom of association with others, including the right to form and join trade unions for the protection of his interests.
2. No restrictions may be placed on the exercise of this right other than those which are prescribed by law and which are necessary in a democratic society in the interests of national security or public safety, public order (ordre public), the protection of public health or morals or the protection of the rights and freedoms of others. This article shall not prevent the imposition of lawful restrictions on members of the armed forces and of the police in their exercise of this right.
3. Nothing in this article shall authorize States Parties to the International Labour Organisation Convention of 1948 concerning Freedom of Association and Protection of the Right to Organize to take legislative measures which would prejudice, or to apply the law in such a manner as to prejudice, the guarantees provided for in that Convention.

Article 23

1. The family is the natural and fundamental group unit of society and is entitled to protection by society and the State.
2. The right of men and women of marriageable age to marry and to found a family shall be recognized.

3. No marriage shall be entered into without the free and full consent of the intending spouses.
4. States Parties to the present Covenant shall take appropriate steps to ensure equality of rights and responsibilities of spouses as to marriage, during marriage and at its dissolution. In the case of dissolution, provision shall be made for the necessary protection of any children.

Article 24

1. Every child shall have, without any discrimination as to race, colour, sex, language, religion, national or social origin, property or birth, the right to such measures of protection as are required by his status as a minor, on the part of his family, society and the State.
2. Every child shall be registered immediately after birth and shall have a name.
3. Every child has the right to acquire a nationality.

Article 25

Every citizen shall have the right and the opportunity, without any of the distinctions mentioned in article 2 and without unreasonable restrictions:

(a) To take part in the conduct of public affairs, directly or through freely chosen representatives;
(b) To vote and to be elected at genuine periodic elections which shall be by universal and equal suffrage and shall be held by secret ballot, guaranteeing the free expression of the will of the electors;
(c) To have access, on general terms of equality, to public service in his country.

Article 26

All persons are equal before the law and are entitled without any discrimination to the equal protection of the law. In this respect, the law shall prohibit any discrimination and guarantee to all persons equal and effective protection against discrimination on any ground such as race, colour, sex, language, religion, political or other opinion, national or social origin, property, birth or other status.

Article 27

In those States in which ethnic, religious or linguistic minorities exist, persons belonging to such minorities shall not be denied the right, in community with the other members of their group, to enjoy their own culture, to profess and practice their own religion, or to use their own language.

PART IV

Article 28

1. There shall be established a Human Rights Committee (hereafter referred to in the present Covenant as the Committee). It shall consist of eighteen members and shall carry out the functions hereinafter provided.
2. The Committee shall be composed of nationals of the States Parties to the present Covenant who shall be persons of high moral character and recognized competence in the field of human rights, consideration being given to the usefulness of the participation of some persons having legal experience.
3. The members of the Committee shall be elected and shall serve in their personal capacity.

. . . .

Article 41

1. A State Party to the present Covenant may at any time declare under this article that it recognizes the competence of the Committee to receive and consider communications to the effect that a State Party claims that another State Party is not fulfilling its obligations under the present Covenant. Communications under this article may be received and considered only if submitted by a State Party which has made a declaration recognizing in regard to itself the competence of the Committee. No communication shall be received by the Committee if it concerns a State Party which has not made such a declaration. Communications received under this article shall be dealt with in accordance with the following procedure:
   (a) If a State Party to the present Covenant considers that another State Party is not giving effect to the provisions of the present Covenant, it may, by written communication, bring the matter to the attention of that State Party. Within three months after the receipt of the communication the receiving State shall afford the State which sent the

communication an explanation, or any other statement in writing clarifying the matter which should include, to the extent possible and pertinent, reference to domestic procedures and remedies taken, pending, or available in the matter;

(b) If the matter is not adjusted to the satisfaction of both States Parties concerned within six months after the receipt by the receiving State of the initial communication, either State shall have the right to refer the matter to the Committee, by notice given to the Committee and to the other State. …

Article 42

1.

(a) If a matter referred to the Committee in accordance with article 41 is not resolved to the satisfaction of the State Parties concerned, the Committee may, with the prior consent of the States Parties concerned, appoint an ad hoc Conciliation Commission (hereinafter referred to as the Commission). The good offices of the Commission shall be made available to the States Parties concerned with a view to an amicable solution of the matter on the basis of respect for the present Covenant. . . .

NOTE

1. The United Nations International Covenant On Civil And Political Rights, 999 U.N.T.S. at 171 (1966).

Appendix E

Universal Declaration on the Human Genome and Human Rights

The General Conference,

Recalling that the Preamble of UNESCO's Constitution refers to "the democratic principles of the dignity, equality and mutual respect of men," rejects any "doctrine of the inequality of men and races," stipulates "that the wide diffusion of culture, and the education of humanity for justice and liberty and peace are indispensable to the dignity of men and constitute a sacred duty which all the nations must fulfil in a spirit of mutual assistance and concern," proclaims that "peace must be founded upon the intellectual and moral solidarity of mankind," and states that the Organization seeks to advance "through the educational and scientific and cultural relations of the peoples of the world, the objectives of international peace and of the common welfare of mankind for which the United Nations Organization was established and which its Charter proclaims,"

Solemnly recalling its attachment to the universal principles of human rights, affirmed in particular in the Universal Declaration of Human Rights of 10 December 1948 and in the two International United Nations Covenants on Economic, Social and Cultural Rights and on Civil and Political Rights and on Civil and Political Rights of 16 December 1966. . . . [1]

Recognizing that research on the human genome and the resulting applications open up vast prospects for progress in improving the health of individuals and of humankind as a whole, but emphasizing that such research should fully respect human dignity, freedom and human rights, as well as the prohibition of all forms of discrimination based on genetic characteristics,

Proclaims the principles that follow and *adopts* the present Declaration.

A. HUMAN DIGNITY AND THE HUMAN GENOME

Article 1

The human genome underlies the fundamental unity of all members of the human family, as well as the recognition of their inherent dignity and diversity. In a symbolic sense, it is the heritage of humanity.

Article 2

(a) Everyone has a right to respect for their dignity and for their rights regardless of their genetic characteristics.
(b) That dignity makes it imperative not to reduce individuals to their genetic characteristics and to respect their uniqueness and diversity.

Article 3

The human genome, which by its nature evolves, is subject to mutations. It contains potentialities that are expressed differently according to each individual's natural and social environment including the individual's state of health, living conditions, nutrition and education.

Article 4

The human genome in its natural state shall not give rise to financial gains.

B. RIGHTS OF THE PERSONS CONCERNED

Article 5

(a) Research, treatment or diagnosis affecting an individual's genome shall be undertaken only after rigorous and prior assessment of the potential risks and benefits pertaining thereto and in accordance with any other requirement of national law.
(b) In all cases, the prior, free and informed consent of the person concerned shall be obtained. If the latter is not in a position to consent, consent or authorization shall be obtained in the manner prescribed by law, guided by the person's best interest.

(c) The right of each individual to decide whether or not to be informed of the results of genetic examination and the resulting consequences should be respected.
(d) In the case of research, protocols shall, in addition, be submitted for prior review in accordance with relevant national and international research standards or guidelines.
(e) If according to the law a person does not have the capacity to consent, research affecting his or her genome may only be carried out for his or her direct health benefit, subject to the authorization and the protective conditions prescribed by law. Research which does not have an expected direct health benefit may only be undertaken by way of exception, with the utmost restraint, exposing the person only to a minimal risk and minimal burden and if the research is intended to contribute to the health benefit of other persons in the same age category or with the same genetic condition, subject to the conditions prescribed by law, and provided such research is compatible with the protection of the individual's human rights.

Article 6

No one shall be subjected to discrimination based on genetic characteristics that is intended to infringe or has the effect of infringing human rights, fundamental freedoms and human dignity.

Article 7

Genetic data associated with an identifiable person and stored or processed for the purposes of research or any other purpose must be held confidential in the conditions set by law.

Article 8

Every individual shall have the right, according to international and national law, to just reparation for any damage sustained as a direct and determining result of an intervention affecting his or her genome.

Article 9

In order to protect human rights and fundamental freedoms, limitations to the principles of consent and confidentiality may only be prescribed by law, for compelling reasons within the bounds of public international law and the international law of human rights.

C. RESEARCH ON THE HUMAN GENOME

Article 10

No research or research applications concerning the human genome, in particular in the fields of biology, genetics and medicine, should prevail over respect for the human rights, fundamental freedoms and human dignity of individuals or, where applicable, of groups of people.

Article 11

Practices which are contrary to human dignity, such as reproductive cloning of human beings, shall not be permitted. States and competent international organizations are invited to co-operate in identifying such practices and in taking, at national or international level, the measures necessary to ensure that the principles set out in this Declaration are respected.

Article 12

(a) Benefits from advances in biology, genetics and medicine, concerning the human genome, shall be made available to all, with due regard for the dignity and human rights of each individual.
(b) Freedom of research, which is necessary for the progress of knowledge, is part of freedom of thought. The applications of research, including applications in biology, genetics and medicine, concerning the human genome, shall seek to offer relief from suffering and improve the health of individuals and humankind as a whole.

D. CONDITIONS FOR THE EXERCISE OF SCIENTIFIC ACTIVITY

Article 13

The responsibilities inherent in the activities of researchers, including meticulousness, caution, intellectual honesty and integrity in carrying out their research as well as in the presentation and utilization of their findings, should be the subject of particular attention in the framework of research on the human genome, because of its ethical and social implications. Public and private science policy-makers also have particular responsibilities in this respect.

Article 14

States should take appropriate measures to foster the intellectual and material conditions favourable to freedom in the conduct of research on the human genome and to consider the ethical, legal, social and economic implications of such research, on the basis of the principles set out in this Declaration.

Article 15

States should take appropriate steps to provide the framework for the free exercise of research on the human genome with due regard for the principles set out in this Declaration, in order to safeguard respect for human rights, fundamental freedoms and human dignity and to protect public health. They should seek to ensure that research results are not used for non-peaceful purposes.

Article 16

States should recognize the value of promoting, at various levels, as appropriate, the establishment of independent, multidisciplinary and pluralist ethics committees to assess the ethical, legal and social issues raised by research on the human genome and its application.

E. SOLIDARITY AND INTERNATIONAL COOPERATION

Article 17

States should respect and promote the practice of solidarity towards individuals, families and population groups who are particularly vulnerable to or affected by disease or disability of a genetic character. They should foster, *inter alia*, research on the identification, prevention and treatment of genetically based and genetically influenced diseases, in particular rare a well as endemic diseases which affect large numbers of the world's population.

Article 18

States should make every effort, with due and appropriate regard for the principles set out in this Declaration, to continue fostering the international dissemination of scientific knowledge concerning the human genome, human diversity and genetic research and, in that regard, to foster scientific and cultural co-operation, particularly between industrialized and developing countries.

Article 19

(a) In the framework of international co-operation with developing countries, States should seek to encourage measures enabling:
   (i) Assessment of the risks and benefits pertaining to research on the human genome to be carried out and abuse to be prevented;
   (ii) The capacity of developing countries to carry out research on human biology and genetics, taking into consideration their specific problems, to be developed and strengthened;
   (iii) Developing countries to benefit from the achievements of scientific and technological research so that their use in favour of economic and social progress can be to the benefit of all;
   (iv) The free exchange of scientific knowledge and information in the areas of biology, genetics and medicine to be promoted.

(b) Relevant international organizations should support and promote the initiatives taken by States for the above-mentioned purposes.

F. PROMOTION OF THE PRINCIPLES SET OUT IN THE DECLARATION

Article 20

States should take appropriate measures to promote the principles set out in the Declaration, through education and relevant means, inter alia through the conduct of research and training in interdisciplinary fields and through the promotion of education in bioethics, at all levels, in particular for those responsible for science policies.

Article 21

States should take appropriate measures to encourage other forms of research, training and information dissemination conducive to raising the awareness of society and all of its members of their responsibilities regarding the fundamental issues relating to the defense of human dignity which may be raised by research in biology, in genetics and in medicine, and its applications. They should also undertake to facilitate on this subject an open international discussion, ensuring the free expression of various sociocultural, religious and philosophical opinions.

G. IMPLEMENTATION OF THE DECLARATION

Article 22

States should make every effort to promote the principles set out in this Declaration and should, by means of all appropriate measures, promote their implementation.

Article 23

States should take appropriate measures to promote, through education, training and information dissemination, respect for the above-mentioned principles and to foster their recognition and effective application. States should also encourage exchanges and networks among independent ethics committees, as they are established, to foster full collaboration.

Article 24

The International Bioethics Committee of UNESCO should contribute to the dissemination of the principles set out in this Declaration and to the further examination of issues raised by their applications and by the evolution of the technologies in question. It should organize appropriate consultations with parties concerned, such as vulnerable groups. It should make recommendations, in accordance with UNESCO's statutory procedures, addressed to the General Conference and give advice concerning the follow-up of this Declaration, in particular regarding the identification of practices that could be contrary to human dignity, such as germ-line interventions.

Article 25

Nothing in this Declaration may be interpreted as implying for any state, group or person any claim to engage in any activity or to perform any act contrary to human rights and fundamental freedoms, including the principles set out in this Declaration.

NOTE

1. Universal Declaration on The Human Genome and Human Rights, UNESCO General Conference Resolution 29C/17 UNESCO.GC, 29th Sess. (1997).

Appendix F

Additional Universal Instruments Relating to Human Rights Prepared by the Office of the High Commissioner for Human Rights of the United Nations

World Conference On Human Rights And Millennium Assembly:

Vienna Declaration and Programme of Action.[1]
United Nations Millennium Declaration.

The Right Of Self-Determination:

United Nations Declaration on the Granting of Independence to Colonial Countries and Peoples.
General Assembly resolution 1803 (XVII) of 14 December 1962, "Permanent sovereignty over natural resources."
International Convention against the Recruitment, Use, Financing and Training of Mercenaries.

Rights Of Indigenous Peoples And Minorities:

Declaration on the Rights of Indigenous Peoples.
Indigenous and Tribal Peoples Convention, 1989 (No. 169).
Declaration on the Rights of Persons Belonging to National or Ethnic, Religious and Linguistic Minorities.

Prevention Of Discrimination:

Equal Remuneration Convention, 1951 (No. 100).
Discrimination (Employment and Occupation) Convention, 1958 (No. 111).
International Convention on the Elimination of all Forms of Racial Discrimination (ICERD).

Declaration on Race and Racial Prejudice.
Convention against Discrimination in Education.
Protocol Instituting a Conciliation and Good Offices Commission to be responsible for seeking a settlement of any disputes which may arise between States Parties to the Convention against Discrimination in Education.
Declaration on the Elimination of All Forms of Intolerance and of Discrimination Based on Religion or Belief.
World Conference against Racism, 2001 (Durban Declaration and Programme of Action).

Rights Of Women:

Convention on the Elimination of All Forms of Discrimination against Women (CEDAW).
Optional Protocol to the Convention on the Elimination of All Forms of Discrimination against Women (CEDAW-OP).
Declaration on the Protection of Women and Children in Emergency and Armed Conflict.
Declaration on the Elimination of Violence against Women.

Rights Of The Child:

Convention on the Rights of the Child (CRC).
Optional Protocol to the Convention on the Rights of the Child on the sale of children, child prostitution and child pornography (CRC-OPSC).
Optional Protocol to the Convention on the Rights of the Child on the involvement of children in armed conflict (CRC-OPAC).
Minimum Age Convention, 1973 (No. 138).
Worst Forms of Child Labour Convention, 1999 (No. 182).

Rights Of Older Persons:

United Nations Principles for Older Persons.

Rights Of Persons With Disabilities:

Convention on the Rights of Persons with Disabilities.
Optional Protocol to the Convention on the Rights of Persons with Disabilities.
Declaration on the Rights of Mentally Retarded Persons.
Declaration on the Rights of Disabled Persons.

Principles for the protection of persons with mental illness and the improvement of mental health care.
Standard Rules on the Equalization on Opportunities for Persons with Disabilities.

Human Rights In The Administration Of Jutice: Protection Of Persons Subjected To Detention Or Imprisonment:

United Nations Standard Minimum Rules for the Treatment of Prisoners (the Nelson Mandela Rules).
Basic Principles for the Treatment of Prisoners.
Body of Principles for the Protection of All Persons under Any Form of Detention or Imprisonment.
United Nations Rules for the Protection of Juveniles Deprived of their Liberty.
Declaration on the Protection of All Persons from Being Subjected to Torture and Other Cruel, Inhuman or Degrading Treatment or Punishment.
Convention against Torture and Other Cruel, Inhuman or Degrading Treatment or Punishment (CAT).
Optional Protocol to the Convention against Torture and Other Cruel, Inhuman or Degrading Treatment or Punishment (OPCAT).
Principles of Medical Ethics relevant to the Role of Health Personnel, particularly Physicians, in the Protection of Prisoners and Detainees against Torture and Other Cruel, Inhuman or Degrading Treatment or Punishment.
Principles on the Effective Investigation and Documentation of Torture and Other Cruel, Inhuman or Degrading Treatment or Punishment.
Safeguards guaranteeing protection of the rights of those facing the death penalty.
Code of Conduct for Law Enforcement Officials.
Basic Principles on the Use of Force and Firearms by Law Enforcement Officials.
United Nations Standard Minimum Rules for Non-Custodial Measures (The Tokyo Rules).
United Nations Standard Minimum Rules for the Administration of Juvenile Justice (The Beijing Rules).
Guidelines for Action on Children in the Criminal Justice System.
United Nations Guidelines for the Prevention of Juvenile Delinquency (The Riyadh Guidelines).
Declaration of Basic Principles of Justice for Victims of Crime and Abuse of Power.
Basic Principles on the Independence of the Judiciary.
Basic Principles on the Role of Lawyers.
Guidelines on the Role of Prosecutors.

Principles on the Effective Prevention and Investigation of Extra-Legal, Arbitrary and Summary Executions.
Declaration on the Protection of All Persons from Enforced Disappearance.
Basic Principles and Guidelines on the Right to a Remedy and Reparation.
International Convention for the Protection of All Persons from Enforced Disappearance.
United Nations Rules for the Treatment of Women Prisoners and Non-Custodial Measures for Women Offenders (the Bangkok Rules).
Updated Set of principles for the protection and promotion of human rights through action to combat impunity.

Social Welfare, Progress And Development:

Declaration on Social Progress and Development.
Universal Declaration on the Eradication of Hunger and Malnutrition.
Declaration on the Use of Scientific and Technological Progress in the Interests of Peace and for the Benefit of Mankind.
Declaration on the Right of Peoples to Peace.
Declaration on the Right to Development.
Universal Declaration on the Human Genome and Human Rights.
Universal Declaration on Cultural Diversity.

Promotion And Protection Of Human Rights:

Principles relating to the status of national institutions (The Paris Principles).
Declaration on the Right and Responsibility of Individuals, Groups and Organs of Society to Promote and Protect Universally Recognized Human Rights and Fundamental Freedoms.
United Nations Declaration on Human Rights Education and Training.

Marriage:

Convention on Consent to Marriage, Minimum Age for Marriage and Registration of Marriages.
Recommendation on Consent to Marriage, Minimum Age for Marriage and Registration of Marriages.

Right To Health:

Declaration of Commitment on HIV/AIDS.

Right To Work And To Fair Conditions Of Employment:

Employment Policy Convention, 1964 (No. 122).

Freedom Of Association:

Freedom of Association and Protection of the Right to Organize Convention, 1948 (No. 87).
Right to Organize and Collective Bargaining Convention, 1949 (No. 98).

Slavery, Slavery-Like Practices And Forced Labour:

Slavery Convention.
Protocol amending the Slavery Convention signed at Geneva on 25 September 1926.
Supplementary Convention on the Abolition of Slavery, the Slave Trade, and Institutions and Practices Similar to Slavery.
Forced Labour Convention, 930 (No. 29).
Protocol of 2014 to the Forced Labour Convention, 1930.
Abolition of Forced Labour Convention, 1957 (No. 105).
Convention for the Suppression of the Traffic in Persons and of the Exploitation of the Prostitution of Others.
Protocol to Prevent, Suppress and Punish Trafficking in Persons, Especially Women and Children, supplementing the United Nations Convention against Transnational Organized Crime.

Rights Of Migrants:

International Convention on the Protection of the Rights of All Migrant Workers and Members of Their Families (ICPMW).
Protocol against the Smuggling of Migrants by Land, Sea and Air, supplementing the United Nations Convention against Transnational Organized Crime.

Nationality, Statelessness, Asylum And Refugees:

Convention on the Reduction of Statelessness.
Convention relating to the Status of Stateless Persons.
Convention relating to the Status of Refugees.
Protocol relating to the Status of Refugees.
Declaration on the Human Rights of Individuals who are not nationals of the country in which they live.

War Crimes And Crimes Against Humanity, Including Genocide:

Convention on the Prevention and Punishment of the Crime of Genocide.

Convention on the Non-Applicability of Statutory Limitations to War Crimes and Crimes against Humanity.

Principles of international co-operation in the detection, arrest, extradition and punishment of persons guilty of war crimes and crimes against humanity.

Statute of the International Tribunal for the Former Yugoslavia.

Statute of the International Tribunal for Rwanda.

Rome Statute of the International Criminal Court.

Humanitarian Law:

Geneva Convention relative to the Treatment of Prisoners of War.

Geneva Convention relative to the Protection of Civilian Persons in Time of War.

Protocol Additional to the Geneva Conventions of 12 August 1949, and relating to the Protection of Victims of International Armed Conflicts (Protocol I).

Protocol Additional to the Geneva Conventions of 12 August 1949, and relating to the Protection of Victims of Non-International Armed Conflicts (Protocol II).

NOTE

1. In 2018, the Office of The High Commissioner for Human Rights of the United Nations prepared this comprehensive—although non-exhaustive—listing of other significant universal instruments relating to Human Rights which complement and strengthen the core of the International Bill of Rights: the Universal Declaration of Human Rights and the Covenants of Economic, Social and Cultural Rights and for Civil and Political Rights. This listing is to be found at http://www.ohchr.org/EN/ProfessionalInterest/Pages/ UniversalHumanRightsInstruments.aspx. An alternate citation is http://legal.org/aol/handbook.html (Codification Division, Office of Legal Affairs, United Nations).

Bibliography

Books

Ackerman, Bruce. 2014. We the People: The Civil Rights Revolution. Cambridge, MA: Harvard University Press.
Alexy, Robert and Julian Rivers. 2010. A Theory of Constitutional Rights. Oxford: University of Oxford Press.
Barak, Aharon. 2012. Proportionality: Constitutional Rights and their Limitations. Cambridge: University of Cambridge Press.
Barak, Aharon. 2015. Human Dignity: The Constitutional Value and the Constitutional Right. Cambridge: University of Cambridge Press.
Bastar, Kemal. 1998. The Concept of the Common Heritage of Mankind in International Law. The Netherlands: Dordecht.
Bedajaoui, Mohammed. 1979. Towards a New International Economic Order. New York: Holmes & Meier.
Biggs, Hazel. 2001. Euthanasia, Death with Dignity and the Law. London: Bloomsbury.
Biukovic, Ljiljana and Pitman B. Potter, eds. 2017. Local Engagement with International Economic Law and Human Rights. London: Edward Elgar Publishing.
Boddice, Rob. 2017. Pain. Oxford: University of Oxford Press.
Breyer, Stephen. 2015. The Court and the World: American Law and the New Global Realties. New York: Barnes & Noble.
Brombert, Victor. 2013. Musings on Mortality. Chicago: University of Chicago Press.
Burgorgue-Larsen, Laurence and Amaya Ubeda de Torres. 2011. The Inter-American Court of Human Rights: Case Law and Commentary. Oxford: University of Oxford Press.
Capps, Patrick. 2009. Human Dignity and the Foundations of International Law. Oxford: Hart Publishing.
Cardozo, Benjamin. 1921. The Nature of the Judicial Process. New Haven, CT: Yale University Press.
Christofferson, Jonas and Mikael Rask Madsen. 2011. The European Court of Human Rights between Law and Politics. Oxford: University of Oxford Press.

Cohen, I. Glenn, ed. 2014. The Globalization of Health Care: Legal and Ethical Issues. New York: Oxford University Press.
Cotesta, Vittorio. 2012. Global Society and Human Rights. Leiden: Brill.
Davis, Dennis. 2017. An Enquiry into the Existence of Global Values through the Laws of Comparative-Constitutional Law. Oxford: Hart Publishing.
Dillon, Robert S., ed. 1998. Dignity, Character, and Self Respect. London: Routledge.
Dolgin, Janet L. and Lois L. Shepherd, eds. 2013. Bioethics and the Law. New York: Aspen Publishers.
Dupre, Catherine. 2015. The Age of Dignity: Human Rights and Constitutionalism. Oxford: Hart Publishing.
Ehrenreich, Barbara. 2018. Natural Causes: An Epidemic of Wellness, the Certainty of Dying, and Killing Ourselves to Live Longer. New York: Grand Central Publishing.
Epstein, Richard. 1997. Mortal Peril: Our Inalienable Right to Health Care? Boston: Addison-Wesley Publishing.
Ernst, Carl W. 2013. Islamophobia in America: The Anatomy of Intolerance. New York: Springer.
Ferngren, Gary B. 2009. Medicine and Health Care in Early Christianity. Baltimore, MD: Johns Hopkins University.
Fletcher, John. 1966. Situation Ethics: The New Morality. Louisville, KY: Westminster John Knox.
Foley, Elizabeth. 2011. The Law of Life and Death. Cambridge, MA: Harvard University Press.
Frankfort, Harry G. 2004. The Reasons of Love. Princeton, NJ: University of Princeton.
Fredman, Sandra. 2008. Human Rights Transformed: Positive Rights and Positive Duties. Oxford: University of Oxford Press.
Fuller, Lon L. 1964. The Morality of Law. New Haven, CT: Yale University Press.
Gawande, Atul. 2014. Being Mortal. New York: Metropolitan Books.
Glover, Jonathan. 1999. Humanity: A Moral History of the Twentieth Century. New Haven, CT: Yale University Press.
Goldsmith, Jack and Eric Posner. 2015. The Limits of International Law. Oxford: University of Oxford Press.
Gorsuch, Neil M. 2006. The Future of Assisted Suicide and Euthanasia. Princeton, NJ: University of Princeton Press.
Griffiths, John, Helen Weyers and Maurice Adams. 2008. Euthanasia and Law in Europe. Oxford: Hart Publishing.
Groves, Richard F. and Hennriette A. Klauser. 2009. The American Book of Living and Dying: Lessons in Healing Spiritual Pain. 2009. Berkeley, CA: Celestial Arts.
Guild, Elspeth and Guillaume Lesieur. 1998. The European Court of Justice on the European Convention on Human Rights. The Netherlands: Brill.
Hagger, Lynn and Simon Woods, eds. 2013. A Good Death? Law and Ethics in Practice. Farnham, UK: Ashgate.
Hauerwas, Stanley. 1990. God, Medicine, and Suffering. Grand Rapids, MI: W. B. Eerdemans.

Henkin, Louis. 1978. The Rights of Man Today. New York: Yeshiva University Press.
Herring, Jonathan. 2013. Caring and the Law. Oxford: Hart Publishing.
Hestermeyer, Holger. 2007. Human Rights and the WTO: The Case of Patents and Access to Medicines. Oxford: University of Oxford Press.
Hicks, Donna. 2011. Dignity: The Essential Role It Plays in Resolving Conflict. New Haven, CT: Yale University Press.
Hulsroj, Peter. 2013. The Principle of Proportionality. New York: Springer.
Humphry, Derek. 2010. Final Exit. 3rd ed. New York: Penguin Random House.
James, Stephen. 2007. Universal Rights. New York: LFB.
Janis, Mark. 1999. An Introduction to International Law. New York: Aspen Publishers.
Kalanithi, Paul. 2016. When Breath Becomes Air. New York: Random House.
Kälin, Walter and Jörg Künzli. 2004. The Law of International Human Rights Protection. Oxford: University of Oxford Press.
Kass, Leon. 2002. Life, Liberty, and the Defense of Dignity. San Francisco: Encounter Books.
Kateb, George. 2013. Human Dignity. Cambridge, MA: Harvard University Press.
Kissinger, Henry. 2014. World Order. New York: Penguin Press.
Kolnai, Aurel. 1976. Dignity. Cambridge: University of Cambridge Press.
Kraynack, Robert and Glenn Tinder, eds. 2003. In Defense of Human Dignity: Essays for Our Times. South Bend, IN: Notre Dame University Press.
Lagon, Mark and Anthony Clark Arend. 2014. Human Dignity and the Future of Global Institutions. Washington, D.C.: Georgetown University Press.
Lindsay, Ronald A. 2008. Future Bioethics: Overcoming Taboos, Myths, and Dogmas. Amherst, NY: Prometheus.
Llewellyn, Karl. 1960. The Common Law Tradition. Boston: Little, Brown & Co.
Ludwikowski, Rett and Gisbert H. Franz. 2002. Human Rights and Fundamental Freedoms. New York: Oceana.
Lutz-Bachmann, Mathias. 2016. Human Rights, Human Dignity and Cosmopolitan Ideals. London: Routledge.
Lynn, Joanne. 2004. Sick to Death and Not Going to Take It Anymore! Berkeley: University of California Press.
McDougal, Myres, Harold D. Lasswell, and Lung-Chu Chen. 1980. Human Rights and World Public Order. New Haven, CT: Yale University Press.
Meier, Benjamin M. 2011. The Highest Attainable Standard: The World Health Organization, Global Health Governance and the Contentious Politics of Human Rights. Charleston, SC: Biblio Bazaar.
Meier, Benjamin M. and Lawrence O. Gostin. 2018. Human Rights in Global Health: Rights-Based Governance for a Globalizing World. Oxford: University of Oxford Press.
Murphy, Therese. 2013. Health and Human Rights. Oxford: Hart Publishing.
Murray, Charles. 1994. The Bell Curve. New York: Free Press.
Nagel, David. Needless Suffering: How Society Fails those with Chronic Pain. Lebanon, NH: University of New England Press.

Negri, Stefania, ed. 2012. Self-Determination, Dignity and End-of-Life Care: Regulating Advance Directives in International and Comparative Perspectives. Leiden, Belgium: Nijhoff.

Newton, Michael and Larry May. 2014. Proportionality in International Law. Oxford: University of Oxford Press.

Noonan, John. 1976. Persons and Masks of Law. New York: Farrar, Straus & Giroux.

Nozick, Robert. 1974. Anarchy, State and Utopia. New York: Basic Books.

Nuland, Sherwin B. 1994. How Do We Die: Reflections on Life's Final Chapter. New York: Vintage Books.

Orakhelashvili, Alexander. 2006. Pre-Emptory Norms in International Law. Oxford: University of Oxford Press.

Pellegrino, Edmund D. and David C. Thomasma. 1988. For the Patient's Own Good: The Restoration of Beneficence in Health Care. Oxford: University of Oxford Press.

Poo, Ai-Jen. 2015. The Age of Dignity: Preparing for the Elder Boom in a Changing America. New York: The Free Press.

Posner, Richard A. 2008. How Judges Think. Cambridge, MA: Harvard University Press.

Posner, Richard A. 1995. Aging and Old Age. Chicago: University of Chicago Press.

Posner, Richard A., ed. 1992. Essential Holmes: Selections from the Letters, Speeches, Judicial Opinions and Other Writings of Oliver Wendell Holmes, Jr. Chicago: University of Chicago Press.

President's Council on Bioethics, ed. 2005. Taking Care: Ethical Caregiving in Our Aging Society. Washington, D.C.: President's Council on Bioethics.

Randall, Fiona and R. S. Downie. 2009. End of Life Choices: Consensus and Controversy. Oxford: University of Oxford Press.

Randall, Fiona and R. S. Downie. 1996. Palliative Care Ethics: A Good Companion. Oxford: University of Oxford Press.

Rawls, John. 1971. A Theory of Justice. Cambridge, MA: Harvard University Press.

Roberts, Christopher. 2014. The Contentious History of the International Bill of Human Rights. Cambridge: University of Cambridge Press.

Rosen, Michael. 2012. Dignity: Its History and Meaning. Cambridge, MA: Harvard University Press.

Rossi, Christopher. 1999. Equity and International Law. Leiden, Belgium: Nijhoff.

Roth, Martin. 1993. Ageing and the Aged in Contemporary Society. Bloomington: Indiana University Press.

Sangiovanni, Andrea. 2017. Humanity without Dignity. Cambridge, MA: Harvard University Press.

Saunders, Cicely and Robert Kastenbaum, eds. 1997. Hospice Care on the International Scene. New Rochelle, NY: Mary Ann Liebert, Inc.

Schillace, Brandy. 2015. Death's Summer Coat: What the History of Death and Dying Can Tell Us about Life and Living. New York: Pegasus Books.

Schmidt, Pierre. 2017. Access to Justice and International Organizations: The Case of Individual Victims of Human Rights Violations. London: Edward Elgar Publishing.

Shelton, Dinah. 2005. Remedies in International Human Rights Law. Oxford: University of Oxford Press.

Shepherd, Lois. 2009. If That Ever Happens to Me. Chapel Hill: University of North Carolina Press.

Sieth, Edward and Judy McGregor, eds. 2017. Human Dignity: Establishing Worth and Seeking Solutions. New York: Palgrave-Macmillan.

Smith, Emily. 2017. The Power of Meaning: Crafting a Life That Matters. New York: Crown Publishing.

Smith, George P. 2013. Palliative Care and End of Life Decisions. New York: Palgrave Macmillan.

Smith, George P. 2005. The Christian Religion and Biotechnology: A Search for Principled Decision Making. New York: Springer.

Smith, George P. 2000. Human Rights and Biomedicine. The Netherlands: Kluwer.

Smith, George P. 1993. Bioethics and The Law: Medical, Socio-Legal and Philosophical Direction for a Brave New World. Lanham, MD: University Press of America.

Smith, George P. 1989. Final Choices: Autonomy in Health Care Decisions. Springfield, IL: Charles C. Thomas Publisher.

Smith, George P. 1989. The New Biology: Law, Ethics, and Biotechnology. New York: Plenum.

Smith, Stephen W. 2012. End-of-Life Decisions in Medical Care: Principles and Policies for Regulating The Dying Process. Cambridge: University of Cambridge Press.

Stein, Michael. 2007. The Lonely Patient. New York: HarperCollins.

Steiner, Henry J. and Philip Alston. 1996. International Human Rights in Context: Laws, Politics, Morals. Oxford: University of Oxford Press.

Struck, Peter T. 2016. Divination and Human Nature: A Cognitive History of Intuition in Classic Antiquity. Princeton, NJ: University of Princeton Press.

Sullivan, William. 2005. Eye of The Heart: Knowing the Human Good in the Euthanasia Debate. Toronto: University of Toronto Press.

Sumner, L.W. 2017. Physician-Assisted Death: What Everyone Needs to Know. Oxford: University of Oxford Press.

Szczeklik, Andrzej. 2005. Catharsis: On The Art of Medicine. Chicago: University of Chicago Press.

Tams, Christian J. 2005. Enforcing Obligations Erga Omnes in International Law. Cambridge: University of Cambridge Press.

Thomasma, David C. and Glenn C. Graber. 1991. Euthanasia: Toward an Ethic and Social Policy. New York: Continuum Press.

Thomasma, David C. 1990. Human Life in the Balance. Louisville, KY: Westminster Knox Press.

Tobin, John. 2012. The Right to Health in International Law. Oxford: University of Oxford Press.

Tomuschat, Christian and Jean-Marc Thouvenin, eds. 2006. The Fundamental Rules of International Legal Order: Jus Cogens and Erga Omnes. The Netherlands: Brill.

Trindade, Antonio A. Cancado. 2015. The Construction of a Humanized International Law. The Netherlands: Brill.

Wicks, Elizabeth. 2007. Human Rights and Healthcare. Oxford: Hart Publishing.

Wood, Allen W. 1999. Kant's Ethical Thought. Chicago: University of Chicago Press.

Yamin, Alicia and Sri Gloppen, eds. 2011. Litigating Health Rights: Can Courts Bring More Justice to Health? Cambridge, MA: Harvard University Press.

Book Chapters

Caldwell, Mary Ellen. "'Well-Being': Its Place among Human Rights," in Toward World Order and Human Dignity: Essays in Honor of Myres S. McDougal, eds. W. Michael Reisman and Burns H. Westin (New York: Free Press, 1976), 196.

Campbell, Courtney. "Principilism and Religion: The Law and the Prophets," in A Matter of Principles? Ferment in U.S. Bioethics, ed. Lawrence J. O'Connell (Valley Forge, PA: Trinity Press, 1994), 187.

Canick, Hubert. "Dignity of Man and 'Persona' in Stoic Anthropology: Some Remarks in Cicero's De Officiis I, 105–107," in The Concept of Human Dignity in Human Rights Discourse, eds. David Kretzner and Eckart Klein (The Netherlands: Springer, 2002), 18.

Chaskdson, Arthur. "Comparative Constitutional Perspectives: Human Dignity as a Constitutional Value," in The Concept of Human Dignity in Human Rights Discourse, eds. David Kretzner and Eckhart Klein (The Netherlands: Springer, 2002), 133.

Dicke, Klaus. "The Founding Function of Human Dignity in the Universal Declaration of Human Rights," in The Concept of Human Dignity in Human Rights Discourse, eds. David Kretzner and Eckhart-Klein (The Netherlands: Springer, 2002), Ch. 7.

Follesdal, Andreas. "Subsidarity and The Global Order," in Subsidarity in Comparative Perspective, eds. Augusto Zimmerman and Michele Evans (2014), 207.

Gelernter, David. "The Irreducibly Religious Character of Human Dignity," in Human Dignity and Bioethics, ed. The President's Council on Bioethics (Washington, D.C.: The President's Council on Bioethics, 2008), 532.

Gerwirth, Alan. "Human Dignity as a Basis of Rights," in The Constitution of Rights, eds. Michael J. Meyer and William A. Parent. (Ithaca, NY: Cornell University Press, 1992), 10.

Goos, Christoph. "Restoring Human Dignity in Post-Nazi Germany," in Understanding Human Dignity, ed. Christopher McCudden (Oxford: University of Oxford Press, 2013), Ch. 3.

Grimm, Dieter. "Dignity in a Legal Context: Dignity as an Absolute Right," in Understanding Human Dignity, ed. Christopher McCrudden (Oxford: University of Oxford Press, 2013), 38.

Hanvey, James. "Dignity, Person and Imago Trinitas," in Understanding Human Dignity, ed. Christopher McCudden (Oxford: University of Oxford, 2013), Ch. 11.

Lee, Patrick and Robert P. George. "The Nature and Basis of Human Dignity," in Human Dignity and Bioethics, ed. The President's Council on Bioethics (Washington, D.C.: The President's Council on Bioethics 2008), 410.

McCrudden, Christopher. "In Pursuit of Human Dignity: An Introduction to Current Debates," in Understanding Human Dignity, ed. Christopher McCrudden (Oxford: University of Oxford Press, 2015), 14.

Meyer, Michael. "Dignity as a Modern Value," in The Concept of Human Dignity in Human Rights Discourse, eds. David Kretzner and Eckart Klein (The Netherlands: Springer, 2002), 195.

Mitchell, C. Ben. "The Audacity of The Imago Dei," in Imago Dei: Human Dignity in Ecumenical Perspective, ed. Thomas A. Howard (Washington, D.C.: The Catholic University of America Press, 2013), 79.

Mollers, Christopher. "The Triple Dilemma of Human Dignity: A Case Study," in Understanding Human Dignity, ed. Christopher McCrudden (Oxford: University of Oxford Press, 2015), Ch. 9.

Neuhas, Richard John. "Human Dignity and Public Disclosure," in Human Dignity and Bioethics, ed. The President's Council on Bioethics (Washington, D.C.: The President's Council on Bioethics 2008), 215.

Orbinski, James. "Justice and Global Health," in Law and Global Health, eds. Michael Freeman, Sarah Hawkes, and Belinda Bennett (Oxford: University of Oxford Press, 2014), 11.

Pellegrino, Edmund D. "The Lived Experience of Human Dignity," in Human Dignity and Bioethics, ed. The President's Council on Bioethics (Washington, D.C.: The President's Council on Bioethics 2008), 532.

Picone, Paolo. "The Distinction between Jus Cogens and Obligations Erga Omnes," in The Law of Treaties beyond the Vienna Convention, ed. Enzo Cannizzaro (Oxford: University of Oxford Press, 2011), Ch. 24.

Quill, Timothy E. and Margaret P. Battin. "Excellent Palliative Care as the Standard, Physician Assisted Dying as a Last Resort," in Physician-Assisted Dying: The Case for Palliative Care, eds. Timothy E. Quill and Margaret P. Battin (Baltimore, MD: Johns Hopkins University Press, 2004), 323.

Rosen, Michael. "Dignity: The Case Against," in Understanding Human Dignity, ed. Christopher McCudden (Oxford: University of Oxford Press, 2014), 154.

Smith, George P. "Global Health Law: Aspirational, Paradoxical or Oxymoronic?" in Law and Global Health, eds. Michael Freeman, Sarah Hawkes, and Belinda Bennett. (Oxford: University of Oxford Press, 2014), 24.

Smith, George P. "Access to Health Care: Economic, Medical, Ethical and Socio-Legal Challenges," in Autonomy and Human Rights and Health Care, eds. David N. Weisstub and G. D. Pinto (The Netherlands: Springer, 2008), Ch. 20.

Soskice, Janet. "Human Dignity and the Image of God," in Understanding Human Dignity, ed. Christopher McCudden (Oxford: University of Oxford Press, 2014), Ch. 12.

Tasioulas, John. "Human Dignity and The Foundation of Human Rights," in Understanding Human Dignity, ed. Christopher McCudden (Oxford: University of Oxford Press, 2014), 292.

Weisstub, David. "Honor, Dignity, and The Framing of Multicultural Values," in The Concept of Human Dignity in Human Rights Discourse, eds. David Kretzner and Eckart Klein (The Netherlands, Springer), 270.

Law Review and Other Articles

Adorno, Roberto. "Human Dignity and Human Rights as a Common Ground for Global Bioethics," Journal of Medicine and Philosophy 34:225 (2009).

Agrawal, Manish and Ezekiel J. Emanuel. "Attending to Psychologic Symptoms and Palliative Care," Journal of Clinical Oncology 20:624 (2001).

Alford, Roger P. "Misusing International Sources to Interpret the Constitution," American Journal of International Law 98:57 (2004).

Anstein, Paul. "Self Efficacy as a Mediator of the Relationships between Pain Intensity, Disability and Depression in Chronic Pain Patients Pain," Pain 80:483 (1999).

Ash, Kristina. "U.S. Reservations to the International Covenant on Civil and Political Rights: Credibility and Maximization and Global Influence," Northwestern University Journal of International Human Rights 3:1 (2005).

Astrow, Alan A. "Is Failure to Meet Spiritual Needs Associated with Cancer Patients' Perceptions of Quality of Care and Their Satisfaction with Care?" Journal of Clinical Oncology 25:5753 (2007).

Bianchi, Andrea. "Human Rights and the Use of Jus Cogens," European Journal of International Law 10:491 (2009).

Breitbart, William. "Psychotherapeutic Interventions at the End of Life: A Focus on Mean and Spirituality," Canadian Journal of Psychiatry 48: 336 (2004).

Brennan, William. "The Constitution of the United States," South Texas Law Review 27:433 (1966).

Bumgardner, Cynthia. "Euthanasia and Assisted Suicide in the United States and the Netherlands," Indiana International and Comparative Law Review 10:387 (2000).

Carozza, Paolo G. "The Problematic Applicability of Subsidiarity in International Law," American Journal of Jurisprudence 61:51 (2016).

Carozza, Paolo G. "The Universal Common Good and the Authority of International Law," LOGOS 9:28 (2006).

Carozza. Paolo G. "Subsidiarity as a Structural Principle of International Human Rights Law," American Journal of International Law 97:38 (2003).

Cassell, Eric J. "The Nature of Suffering and the Glory of Medicine," New England Journal of Medicine 301:639 (1982).

Chater, Susan. "Sedation for Intractable Distress in the Dying—A Survey of Experts," Palliative Medicine 12:555 (1998).

Chilton, Adam S. and Eric A. Posner, "The Influence of History on States' Compliance with Human Rights Obligations," Virginia Journal of International Law 56:211 (2016).

Cowan, Jane K. and Julie Billard. "Between Learning and Schooling: The Politics of Human Rights Monitoring at the Universal Periodic Review," Third World Quarterly 36:1175 (2015).

Crosby, John F. "The Twofold Sources of the Divinity of Persons," Faith and Philosophy 18:292 (2001).

Davis, Peggy Cooper. "Little Citizens and their Families," Fordham Urban Law Journal 43:1009 (2016).

de Melo-Martes, Immaculada. "International Dignity in International Policy Documents: A Unified Criteria for Public Policy?" Bioethics 25:37 (2011).

Dineen, Kelly and James DuBois, "Between a Rock and a Hard Place: Can Physicians Prescribe Opioids to Treat Pain Adequately while Avoiding Legal Sanction," American Journal of Law and Medicine 41:531 (2016).

Eberle, Edward J. "Human Dignity, Privacy and Personality in German and American Constitutional Law," Utah Law Review 963 (1997).

Eskridge, William N. "The Marriage Equality Cases and Constitutional Theory," Cato Supreme Court Review 111 (2013).

Faunce, Thomas. "Will Human Rights Subsume Medical Ethics? Intersections in the UNESCO Declarations," Journal of Medical Ethics 31:173 (2004).

Feinberg, Joel. "The Nature and Value of Human Rights," Journal of Value and Inquiry 4:243 (1970).

Finnis, John. "Subsidiarity's Roots and History: Some Observations," American Journal of Jurisprudence 61:133 (2016).

Giannini. Mary M. "The Procreative Power of Dignity: Dignity's Evolution in the Victim's Rights Movement," Drexel Law Review 9:43 (2016).

Glensy, Rex D. "The Right to Dignity," Columbia Human Rights Law Review 67:107 (2011).

Goodman, Maxine D. "Human Dignity in the Supreme Court Jurisprudence," Nebraska Law Review 84:740 (2006).

Gunderman, Richard B. "Is Suffering the Enemy?" Hastings Center Report 32:40 (2002).

Hahn, Harlan. "Antidiscrimination Laws and Social Research on Disability: The Minority Group Perspectives," Behavioral Sciences and The Law 14:41 (1998).

Halenbeck, James. "Terminal Sedation for Intractable Distress: Not Slow Euthanasia but a Prompt Response to Suffering," Western Journal of Medicine 171:222 (1999).

Halvey, Amir. "Medical Futility, Patient Autonomy, and Professional Integrity: Finding the Appropriate Balance," Health Matrix 18:261 (2008).

Hart, Alton. "Hospice Patients' Attitude Regarding Spiritual Discussion with their Doctors," American Journal of Hospital and Hospice Palliation 20:135 (2003).

Heinze, Eric. "Even-Handedness and the Politics of Human Rights," Harvard Human Rights Journal 21:7 (2008).

Henderson, Lynne N. "Legality and Empathy," University of Michigan Law Review 85:1564 (1987).

Henry, Leslie M. "The Jurisprudence of Dignity," University of Pennsylvania Law Review 160:169 (2011).

Hoffman, Leonard. "The Universality of Human Right," Law Quarterly Review 125:416 (2009).

Holmes, Oliver Wendell Jr. "The Path of the Law," Harvard Law Review 10:457 (1897).

Holmes, Seth A. "Screening the Soul: Communication Regarding Spiritual Concerns among Primary Care Physicians and Seriously Ill Patients Approaching the End of Life," American Journal of Hospice and Palliative Medicine 23:25 (2006).

Howard, Rhoda E. and Jack Donnelly. "Human Dignity, Human Rights and Political Regimes," American Political Science Review 80:801 (1986).

Hutchinson, Darren L. "Undignified: The Supreme Court, Racial Justice, and Dignity Claims," Florida Law Review 69:1 (2017).

Hyman, David A. "Does Technology Spell Trouble with a Capital T: Human Dignity and Public Policy," Harvard Journal of Law and Public Policy 27:3 (2003).

Jackson, Vicki. "Constitutional Law in an Age of Proportionality," Yale Law Journal 124:3014 (2015).

Jackson, Vicki. "Constitutional Dialogue and Human Dignity: Sate and Transnational Constitutional Disclosures," Montana Law Review 63:1 (2004).

Jenner, Bruce. "Access to Hospice Care: Expanding Boundaries, Overcoming Boundaries," Hastings Center Report 33:S-1 (2003).

Johnson, Larry. "The United Nations System for the Protection of Human Rights," Georgia Journal of International and Comparative Law 20:363 (1990).

Khuu, Neo. "Obergefell v. Hodges: Kinship, Formation, Interest Convergence and The Future of LGBTQ," University of California, Los Angeles, Law Review 64:184 (2017).

Kirby, Michael D. "Human Rights—The Challenge of the New Technology," Australian Law Journal 60:170 (1986).

Kirby, Michael D. "Human Rights: The Universal Declaration of Human Rights and UNESCO Declaration on Bioethics and Human Rights," Journal of Contemporary Health Law and Policy 25:309 (2009).

Kirby, Michael D. "The New Biology and International Sharing—Lessons from the Life and Work of George P. Smith, II," Indiana Journal of Global Legal Studies 7:425 (2000).

Kirkpatrick, Alexander. "The Caged Bird Sings of Freedom: Why Allowing Sex-Reassignment Surgery for Transgender Life Prisoners Facilities Rehabilitation and Reconciliation," Southern California Law and Social Justice 26:37 (2016).

Kissane, David W. "The Contribution of Demoralization to End of Life Decision-Making," Hastings Center Report 24:21 (2004).

Koh, Harold. "Why Do Nations Obey International Law?" Yale Law Journal 106:2599 (1997).

Koskenniemi, Martti. "The Fate of International Law: Between Technique and Politics," Modern Law Review 70:1 (2007).

Kysel, Ian M. "Domesticating Human Rights Norms in the United States: Considering the Role and Obligations of the Federal Government and Litigants," Georgetown Journal of International Law 46:1009 (2015).

Lindell, Noah B. "The Dignity Canon," Cornell Journal of Law and Public Policy 27:415 (2017).

Lipman, Arthur G. "The Scream of Edward Munch: A Profound Portrayal of Existential Pain," Journal of Pain and Palliative Care Pharmacotherapy 19:1 (2005).

Macklin, Ruth. "Dignity is a Useless Concept," British Medical Journal 217:1419 (2003).

Marlos, Stephen P. "Normative Expansion of the Right to Health and the Proliferation of Human Rights," George Washington University International Law Review 49:97 (2016).

Maruri, Silpa. "Hormone Therapy for Inmates: A Metonym for Transgender Rights," Cornell Journal of Law and Policy 20:807 (2017).

Mashaw, Jerry. "Administrative Due Process: The Question of a Dignitary Theory," Boston University Law Review 61:855 (1981).

McBeth, Adam. "Privatising Human Rights: What Happens to the State's Human Rights Duties When Services Are Privatised?" Melbourne Journal of International Law 5:133 (2004).

McCrudden, Christopher. "Human Dignity and Judicial Interpretation of Human Rights," European Journal of International Law 19:655 (2008).Miller, Karel. "Antidepressant Medicative Use in Palliative Care," American Journal of Hospice and Palliative Medicine 23:127 (2006).

Mohney, Seth. "The Great Power Origins of Human Rights," Michigan Journal of International Law 25:828 (2014).

Morita, Tatsuya. "Terminal Sedation for Existential Distress," American Journal of Hospice and Palliative Care 17:189 (2000).

Nagy, Csongor I. "Do European Union Member States Have to Respect Human Rights? The Application of the European Union's Federal Bill of Rights to Member States," Indiana International and Comparative Law Review 27:1 (2017).

Note. "Constitutional Courts and International Law: Revisiting the Transatlantic Divide," Harvard Law Review 129:1362 (2016).

Onuf, Nicholas G. "Civitas Maxima: Wolff, Vattel and the Fate of Republicanism," American Journal of International Law 88:280 (1994).

Oquendo, Angel R. "The Politicization of Human Rights: Within the Inter-American System and Beyond," New York University Journal of International Law and Politics 50:1 (2017).

Paust, Jordan J. "The Human Right to Die with Dignity," Human Rights Quarterly 17:463 (1995).

Paust, Jordan J. "Human Dignity as a Constitutional Right: A Jurisprudentially Based Inquiry Into Criteria and Content," Howard Law Journal 27:145 (1984).

Pellegrino, Edmund D. "Patient-Physician Autonomy: Conflicting Rights and Obligations in the Physician-Patient Relationship," Journal of Contemporary Health Law and Policy 10:47 (1994).

Perry, Robin. "Balancing Rights? Reconciling the Right to Use Customary Systems of Law with Competing Human Rights in Pursuit of Indigenous Sovereignty," Harvard Human Rights Journal 24:71 (2011).

Piccard, Ann. "The United States' Failure to Ratify the International Covenant on Economic, Social and Cultural Rights: Must the Poor be Always With Us?" St. Mary's Law Review of Minority Rights 13:231 (2010).

Pinker, Stephen. "The Stupidity of Dignity," NEW REPUBLIC 1 (May 28, 2008).

Pope, Thaddeus M. "Legal History of Medical Aid in Dying: Physician Assisted Death in U.S. Courts and Legislatures," New Mexico Law Review 48:267 (2018).

Pustilnik, Amanda C. "Pain as Fact and Heuristic: How Pain Neuroimaging Illuminates Moral Dimensions of Law," Cornell Law Review 97:801 (2012).

Ramsey, Paul. "The Indignity of Death with Dignity," Hastings Center Report 10:47 (1974).

Rao, Neomi. "On the Use and Abuse of Dignity in Constitutional Law," Columbia Journal of European Law 14:210 (2008).

Resnick, Judith and Julie C. Suk. "Adding Insult to Injury: Questioning the Role of Dignity in Conceptions of Sovereignty," Stanford Law Review 55:1921 (2003).

Richardson, Bill. "A New Human Rights Agenda for the U.S.: New Realism, Human Rights and The Rule of Law," Harvard Human Rights Journal 21:1 (2008).

Roberts, Christopher. "Human Rights Law: The (Re)making of an American Story," Minnesota Journal of International Law 26:51 (2017).

Rohan, Patrick. "The Common Law Tradition: 'Just Result' Jurisprudence?" Fordham Law Review 32:51 (1963).

Rousseau, Paul. "Existential Suffering and Palliative Sedation: A Brief Commentary with a Proposal for Clinical Guidelines," American Journal of Hospice and Palliative Care 18:151 (2001).

Rousseau, Paul. "Dying and Terminal Sedation," Clinical Geriatrics 7:18 (1999).

Scalia, Antonin. "The Rule of Law as a Law of Rules," University of Chicago Law Review 56:1183 (1989).

Schachter, Oscar. "Human Dignity as a Normative Concept," American Journal of International Law 77:843 (1983).

Shega, John. "Patients Dying with Dementia: Experience at the End of Life and Impact on Hospice Care," Journal of Pain Symptom Management 35:499 (2008).

Shulziner, Doron. "Human Dignity in Judicial Decisions: Principles of Application and the Rule of Law," Cardozo Journal of International and Comparative Law 23:435 (2017).

Shulziner, Doron. "A Jew's Conception of Human Dignity," Religious Ethics 34:663 (2006).

Shulziner, Doron and Itai Ravinovici. "Human Dignity, Self-Worth and Humiliation: A Comparative Legal-Psychological Approach," Psychology, Public Policy and Law 18:105 (2012).

Siegal, Neil S. "The Virtue of Judicial Statesmanship," Texas Law Review 86:961 (2008).

Smith, George P. "Dignity in Living and Dying," Indiana Journal of Global Legal Studies 25:413 (2018).

Smith, George P. "Dignity as a Normative Standard or as a Value in Global Health Care Decision Making," North Carolina Journal of International Law 42:275 (2017).

Smith, George P. "Applying Bioethics in the 21st Century: Principlism or Situationism," Journal of Contemporary Health Law and Policy 30:37 (2014).

Smith, George P. "Cura Personalis: A Healthcare Delivery Quandary at the End of Life," St. Louis University Journal of Health Law and Policy 7:311 (2014).

Smith, George P. "Gently Into the Good Night: Toward a Compassionate Response to End-Stage Illness," Temple University Journal of Political and Civil Rights 22:475 (2013).
Smith, George P. "Refractory Pain, Existential Suffering and Palliative Care: Releasing the Unbearable Lightness of Being," Cornell Journal of Law and Policy 20:469 (2011).
Smith, George P. "Social Justice and Health Care Management: An Elusive Quest?" Houston Journal of Health Law and Policy 9:1 (2008).
Smith, George P. "Human Rights and Bioethics: Formulating a Universal Right to Health Care or Health Protection," Vanderbilt Journal of Transnational Law 38:1295 (2005).
Smith, George P. "Judicial Decision-Making in the Age of Biotechnology," Notre Dame Journal of Law, Ethics and Public Policy 13:93 (1999).
Smith, George P. "Utility and the Principle of Medical Futility: Safeguarding Autonomy and the Prohibition against Cruel and Unusual Punishment," Journal of Contemporary Health Law and Policy 12:1 (1996).
Smith, George P. "All's Well that Ends Well: Toward a Policy of Assisted Rational Suicide or Merely Enlightened Self-Determination?" University of California-Davis Law Review 22:275 (1989).
Smith, George P. "Terminal Sedation as Palliative Care: Revalidating a Right to a Good Death," Cambridge Quarterly of Healthcare Ethics 7:384 (1989).
Smith, Steven D. "De Moralized: Glucksberg in the Malaise," Michigan Law Review 106:1571 (2008).
Spinck, Jane M. "Dignity Rights," Fordham Urban Law Journal 43:1221 (2016).
Stacks, Helene. "Why Now? Timing and Circumstance of Hastened Deaths," Journal of Pain and Symptom Management 30:215 (2005).
Stahl, Ronit Y. and Ezekiel J. Emanuel. "Physicians, Not Conscripts—Conscientious Objection in Health Care," New England Journal of Medicine 376:1380 (2014).
Stewart, Alec Stone and Judd Matthews. "Proportionality, Balancing and Global Constitutionalism," Columbia Journal of Transnational Law 47:73 (2008).
Stresser, Mark. "Obergefell, Dignity and the Family," Gender, Race and Justice 19:317 (2016).
Sunstein, Cass R. "Due Process Traditionalism," Michigan Law Review 106:1543 (2008).
Symposium. "Dignity Takings and Dignity Restoration," Chicago-Kent Law Review 92:713 (2017).
Tabak, Shana. "Ambivalent Enforcement: International Humanitarian Law at Human Rights Tribunals," Michigan Journal of International Law 37:661 (2016).
Thoreson, Ryan. "The Limits of Moral Limitations: Reconceptualizing 'Morals' in Human Rights Law," Harvard International Law Journal 59:197 (2018).
Tribe, Laurence H. "Lawrence v. Texas: The Fundamental Right That Dare Not Speak ils Name," Harvard Law Journal 117:1892 (2004).
Tribe, Laurence H. "Revising the Rule of Law," New York University Law Review 64:726 (1989).

Van der Wal, Gerrit. "Euthanasia in the Netherlands," British Medical Journal 308:1346 (1994).
Van Hooft, Stan. "The Meanings of Suffering," Hastings Center Report 28:13 (1998).
Waldron, Jeremy. "How Law Protects Dignity," Cambridge Law Journal 71:200 (2012).
Walling, Carrie Booth. "Human Rights Norms: State Sovereignty, and Humanitarian Interventions," Human Rights Quarterly 37:383 (2015).
Whitman, James Q. "How Law Protects Dignity," Cambridge Law Journal 71:200 (2012).
Whitman, James Q. "The Two Western Cultures of Privacy: Dignity Versus Liberty," Yale Law Journal 113:1151 (2004).
Woods, Andrew K. "A Behavioral Approach to Human Rights," Harvard International Law Journal 51:51 (2010).
Yoshino, Kangi. "The Anti-Humiliation Principle and Sex Marriage," Yale Law Journal 123:3077 (2014).
Zaino, Jeanne S. "Self-Respect and Rawlsian Justice," Journal of Politics 60:737 (1998).
Zipursky, Benjamin. "DeShaney and the Jurisprudence of Compassion," New York University Law Review 65:101 (1990).

Court Cases

Baxter v. Montana	354 Mont. 234 (2009)
Brown v. Board of Education	347 U.S. 483 (1954)
Brown v. Plata	131 S. Ct. 1910 (2011)
Carter v. Canada (Attorney General), [2015] SCC5	1 S.C.R. 331
Cruzan v. Missouri Department of Health	497 U.S.261 (1990)
De Shaney v. Winnebago County Department of Social Service	489 U.S. 189 (1988)
Eisenstadt v. Baird	405 U.S. 438 (1972)
Fujii v. State of California	332 U.S. 633 (1948)
Glasser v. United States	315 U.S. 60 (1942)
Gonzales v. Carhart	550 U.S. 124 (2007)
Griswold v. Connecticut	381 U.S. 479 (1965)
Hurd v. Hodge	334 U.S. 24 (1948)
In re Yamashita	327 U.S. 1 (1946)
Jacobellis v. Ohio	378 U.S. 184 (1969)
Lawrence v. Texas	539 U.S. 558 (2003)
Loving v. Virginia	388 U.S. 1 (1967)
Morris v. Brandenburg	376 P. 3d 836 (2016)
Obergefell v. Hodges	135 S. Ct. 2584 (2015)
Oyoma v. California	322 U.S. 633 (1948)
Pennsylvania v. Casey	505 U.S. 833 (1993)
Planned Parenthood v. Southeastern	505 U.S. 833 (1992)
Rodriguez v. British Columbia (Attorney General) [1993]	3 S.C.R. 519
Roper v. Simmons	543 U.S. 551 (2005)
Trop v. Dulles	356 U.S. 86 (1998)

United States v. Smith 18 U.S. 153 (1820)
United States v. Windsor 133 U.S. 2675 (2013)

Physician Assistance at Death State Statutes

California Health and Safety Code, Section 443.1 (2015).
Colorado Revised Statutes, Section 25-48-101 (2016).
District of Columbia Code, Sections 7-66.1-7-661.17 (2017).
Oregon Revised Statutes, Sections 127.800(12), 127.805 (2005).
18 Vermont Statutes Annotated, Chapter 113, Section 5281 (2013).
Washington Revised Code Annotated, Chapter 70.245.160 (West 2009).

United Nations Documents

Charter of The United Nations, October 24, 1945. 1 U.N.T.S., XVI.
International Covenant on Civil and Political Rights. 1966. 999 U.N.T.S. at 171.
International Covenant on Economic, Social and Cultural Rights. 1976. 99 U.N.T.S. at 3.
Universal Declaration on the Human Genome and Human Rights. 1997. UNESCO General Conference Resolution, 29C/17 UNESCO, 29th Sess.
Universal Declaration on Human Rights. 1948. G.A.Res. 217A (III), U.N. Doc. A/810 at 7.
United Human Rights Instruments, A Compilation. United Nations Human Rights, Office of the High Commissioner, www.ohchr.org/EN/Professionallnterest/Pages/UniversalHuman Rightsinstruments.aspx.

Papal Documents

Pope John Paul, II, Centesimus Annus Encyclical, 1991.
Pope John Paul, II, Salvifici Doloris, Apostolic Letter, 1984.
Pope Paul, VI, Populorum Progresso, Encyclical, 1967.
Pope John, XXIII, Pacem Terris Encyclical, 1963.
Pope Pius, XI, Quadragesimo Anno Encyclical, 1931.
Pope Leo, XIII, Rerum Novarum Encyclical, 1891.
All of these papal documents are to be found at www.papalencyclicals.net/.

Magazines and Newspaper Articles

Apuzzo, Matt. 2015. "Transgender Inmate's Hormone Treatment Lawsuit Gets Justice Department Backing," New York Times, April 3.
Brody, Jane. 2016. "To Hasten the End, Some Patients Don't Eat or Drink," New York Times, October 3.
Cha, Ariana Eunjung. 2017. "Alzheimer's Death Rate Rapidly Rising in the U.S.," Washington Post, May 20.
Duncan, Arne and Catherine Lhamon. 2017. "Protecting Transgender Students Is Our Federal Responsibility," Chicago Tribune, February 24.

Esteves, Junno Arocho. 2015. “Holy Year Is a Reminder to Put Mercy before Judgment, Pope Says,” The Catholic Standard, December 17.
Marrin, Minette. 2006. “An Acceptable Way to Arrange Our Death,” The Sunday Times, May 14.
Oster, Randi, R. 2018. “Doctors Should Hear Our Dying Wishes,” Washington Post, April 28.
Sanburn, Josh. 2015. “How Canada’s Right to Die Ruling Could Boost Movement,” Time Magazine, February 6, 2015.
Simpson, Alan K. 2017. “Don’t Let the Anti-LGBT Bigots Win,” New York Times, March 20.
Smith, Wesley J. 2018. “Obliged to Kill: The Assault on Medical Conscience,” The Weekly Standard, March 12.
Stein, Michael. 2016. “Does Kindness Actually Help Us Get Well?” Washington Post, August 14.
“Loved to Death,” The Economist, June 9, 2018.
“The Sorrows of Werther,” The Economist, June 16, 2018.
“The Right to Die,” The Economist, January 27, 2015.
“Final Certainty,” The Economist, June 27, 2015.
“Attitudes Towards Assisted Dying,” The Economist, June 25, 2015.

Index

About the Author

George P. Smith, II, is Professor Emeritus of Law at The Catholic University of America Law School in Washington, D.C., and a Residential Fellow at The Institute for Advanced Study at Indiana University in Bloomington. He began his law-teaching career in 1964 at Indiana University, where he graduated with a B.S. in Business Economics and Public Policy in 1961, a J.D. in 1964, and received an LL.D. degree, *honoris causa,* in 1998. He enjoys both a national and an international reputation as a lecturer and widely published scholar in the fields of Law, Science, and Medicine and Health Law. His postgraduate studies were completed at Columbia University Law School where he received an LL. M. degree in 1975, and at the Yale Law School's Commonwealth Program in Law, Science, and Medicine in 1976–1977 where he was a Senior Fellow. He received an Australian-American Fulbright Foundation Award to the University of New South Wales, Australia, in 1984, was the Parsons Visiting Professor of Law at The University of Sydney in 1998 and 2003, and served as Distinguished Visiting Professor of Law at Macquarie University, Australia, in 2005.

Among his research affiliations which contributed to the preparation of this book are those at: The Solomon Center for Health Law and Policy, Yale University Law School; The Petrie-Flom Center for Health Law Policy, Biotechnology, and Bioethics, Harvard Law School; Australian Institute of Ethics and the Professions, University of Queensland, Australia; Center for Ethics in Culture and The Reilly Center for Science, Technology and Values, Notre Dame University, Indiana; Centre for Medico-Legal Studies, Cardiff University Law School, Wales; Center for Socio-Legal Studies, University of Oxford, England; Centre for the Study of Religion and Politics, University of St. Andrews, Scotland; The Hastings Center, Institute of Society, Ethics and the Life Sciences, New York; The Hoover Institution, Stanford University;

The Max Planck Institute, Heidelberg, Germany; and University of Oxford, Rothermere American Institute, England.

Professor Smith's other related books in the field include: *Palliative Care and End-of-Life Decisions* (2013); *Law and Bioethics: Intersections Along the Mortal Coil* (2012); *Distributive Justice and the New Medicine* (2008); *The Christian Religion and Biotechnology: A Search for Principled Decision-Making* (2005); *Human Rights and Biomedicine* (2000); *Family Values and the New Society* (1998); *Legal and Healthcare Ethics for the Elderly* (1996); *Bioethics and the Law* (1993); *The New Biology* (1989); *Final Choices* (1989); *Medical-Legal Aspects of Cryonics* (1983); *Ethical, Legal and Social Challenges to a Brave New World* (1982) and *Genetics, Ethics and the Law* (1981).

Lightning Source UK Ltd.
Milton Keynes UK
UKHW010605251118
332909UK00008B/499/P

9 781498 584197